About the Author

Wincey Willis has spent her whole life being involved with caring for animals and the environment. She ran a wildlife hospital in County Durham, before doing animal pieces on local radio and TV in the north east of England. She then presented her own series for Granada television called WINCEY'S PETS before moving to London to work at TV-AM, presenting the weather. She has done regular animal and environmental programmes on television. She has written many articles on animals and conservation, as well as two books, *It's Raining Cats and Dogs* and co-written *The Birdwatching Year*. She is currently working as a conservation volunteer involved with turtles.

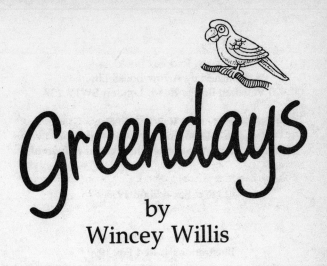

Greendays

by
Wincey Willis

Illustrated by Michael Evans

RED FOX

A Red Fox Book
Published by Arrow Books Limited
20 Vauxhall Bridge Road, London SW1V 2SA

An imprint of the Random Century Group
London, Melbourne, Sydney, Auckland
Johannesburg and agencies throughout the world

Red Fox edition 1990

Designed by Janet Watson

Set in Palatino
by JH Graphics Ltd, Reading

Made and printed in Great Britain by
The Guernsey Press Co Ltd, Guernsey C.I.

ISBN 0 09 972790 0

Introduction

A year and a half ago I was sorting out some photographs to find a suitable one for a magazine article about my childhood holidays. A friend pointed out that there was not a single photograph of me without an animal by my side. Not only was I always with animals but I was also always outdoors.

This has been the pattern of my life. I love the world and the animals and plants we share it with. There are many creatures which are considered to be ugly, but I can see beauty of form and purpose in all that has been designed by nature. We are all interdependent, each living thing a link in the amazing chain of life. If we are not to be responsible for that chain breaking, we must act now. It is OUR world to cherish. We are the caretakers of the future.

A world full of caring people not choosing to see what it is that makes us different, but seeking out that which makes us all the same, would be a wonderful place to start. Begin your part today. I sincerely wish you a future full of happy and green days.

Friend or Foe?

The crow lay dead
and overhead
her mate circled and called.

Come feed our young.

The farmer, shotgun in hand, ten-pence
    cartridge spent,
walked away.
'Damn crows, eat half my crops.'

The caterpillar, trapped in the crow's lifeless
    beak,
wriggled free, and moved off to eat the
    young cabbages.

Greendays

In the spirit of conservation, *Greendays* is a multi-purpose book.

It is a diary without days, so you can use it for more than a year.

It is a general notebook.

It gives you information.

It inspires you to DO something.

I am very keen to hear your ideas on conservation. Please write to me and tell me about your projects, and if you have any new ideas. The address is Wincey Willis, c/o Red Fox, Random Century Ltd, 20 Vauxhall Bridge Road, London, SW1V 2SA. Please enclose an SAE if you would like me to reply.

If you have raised a lot of money for some particular charity or you are starting a massive new project and you would like my help to get some publicity, then let me know. If at all possible I will come along to your event and do what I can.

All proceeds for this book will go to fund the volunteer conservation work I am involved in.

GOOD LUCK AND GOOD GREENING!

Wincey Willis, 1990

Greendays

Unfortunately, despite the contents of this book it has not been possible to use re-cycled paper in its production. I regret this very much. I was advised by the production people that suitable paper to fit their technology was not available. However all the paper used was bought from Scandanivia, where the laws are much stricter than ours, concerning environmental issues. None of the wood pulp comes from the rain forests – it is all locally grown. The conifer plantations are well managed and each felled tree is replaced. The bleaching process uses peroxide rather than the more harmful chlorine which can produce dioxins.

The publishers are currently reviewing their paper buying options and have sent 'green' questionnaires to all their suppliers to ascertain their environmental credentials.

Funding some of your Greendays

If you and your friends are planning to do any kind of work to assist the environment, the Conservation Foundation would like to hear from you.

With Trusthouse Forte, who provide the finance, they have a scheme called the Community Chest. Every month they give grants to groups wanting to fund a particular worthwhile project. The grant can be from £100 to £1000.

You will need to have a good, detailed plan, with photographs and estimates of cost.

For further information and an application form send an SAE to

The Conservation Foundation
1 Kensington Gore
London SW7 2AR

or telephone 071-823 8842.

January

1

For thousands of years, even up to
Norman times, Britain was covered in thick
forest. It took three thousand oak trees to
make one British man-of-war ship. An oak
tree can support up to three hundred
different species.

2

Living things need to eat other living things for
survival. It is called a food chain. Here's one:
rosebush—aphid—hoverfly lavae—centipede—beetle—
frog—grass snake—hedgehog—badger.

3

We can save 135 litres of oil every time we recycle one
tonne of glass. Try not to buy drinks in plastic bottles.
The average family throws away forty kilos of plastic
every year.

4

Don't peel your potatoes! Make sure they are well
scrubbed and eat the whole thing. The skin is rich in
vitamin C, iron and even protein. Try growing your
own. It's easy, and they always seem to taste better.

5

Have a family switch-off day. Don't leave lights on if there is no one in the room. Turn down thermostats on radiators and water heaters.

6

Fancy a snack? Give sweets a miss and buy some brazil nuts. Eating the nuts is one sure way you can help to preserve the trees. If the owner can keep selling the nuts, the tree is more likely to be saved from the logger.

7

Suggest defrosting the fridge today — and help do it. The more ice there is around the freezing compartment the more electricity it takes to keep the contents cold. Cooked and uncooked products should always be wrapped and on separate shelves.

THE BEST THING YOU CAN GIVE IS YOURSELF

We can all find a donation, however small, to give to a worthy cause, and what we give will help. A few pence will pay for food or a vaccine to keep a baby in the Third World alive for one more day. We give because we care and because it makes us feel good ourselves. I know from personal experience that doing as well as giving is much more satisfying. There is nothing wrong with feeling good, especially when what you do to make you feel good is helping to make someone or something else better.

There are many types of voluntary work you can do in your spare time. All the major conservation organizations have local groups which arrange a variety of tasks. Hedge planting, pond cleaning, wall building, path making, litter clearance and wood management are just a few of the tasks for the outdoor types.

If you are not inclined to a spot of muscle building in all weathers, then perhaps you could be useful in organizing or fund-raising, which are equally as important. Many charities have shops where help is always needed. In times of major world disasters, such as earthquakes, the Disasters Emergency Committee, based in London, co-ordinates all the main charities working together. It is through them that all the hundreds of people are gathered together to man the telephone lines during nationwide fund-raising appeals.

Giving a helping hand need not be on a global scale or even as part of a nationwide organization. Being green is about caring, not only for the planet and its plants and animals, but also for the people. Years ago it was normal for people to be born, go to school, work, marry, have children and die, all in the same area. Now it is common for people to travel much more for education and work. Families are often split and grandparents live a long way away. Most older people enjoy the company of younger ones and miss their grandchildren. If your grandparents are not nearby, why don't you seek out some older neighbours your family know? You could do odd jobs for them and sit and talk, and hope that someone is doing the same for your grandparents.

Remember that the voluntary work you do now can be very useful experience, and help when it comes to job hunting.

8

If you like dolphins, think twice before you eat tuna fish. Thousands of dolphins are killed each year by drowning, caught in the nets of tuna fishermen from the USA, Mexico, Panama and Venezuela.

9

Litter is lethal to wildlife. Remember to break the plastic rings which hold drinks cans together before you dispose of them. Thousands of mammals and birds die each year by strangling in these plastic rings or choking on them.

10

There are more than five billion people living on the earth. We must work together to save our planet. The responsibility is yours. Everything we do every day affects the environment. THINK BEFORE YOU ACT.

11

Collect the post this morning. See how many envelopes can be reused. If necessary buy sticky labels, or make your own to cover the old address. Save the stamps for charity fund-raising.

12

Britain has fifteen species of bat. They weigh approximately 5 to 25 grammes and spend ninety per cent of their lives roosting. They are totally harmless to humans, feeding exclusively on insects.

13

The world spends approximately one trillion dollars each year on weapons. Just half a day's worth of this money would be enough to do everything the United Nations say is needed to conserve and replant the world's tropical rainforests.

14

By the year 2050, one in four of all plant species alive today is expected to be extinct. A quarter of all the prescription drugs used in America come from chemicals found in wild plants. What are we going to destroy, before we even know its value?

ALL SPROUTS AREN'T BRUSSELS

You can have a constant supply of fresh crispy vegetables all year round. Sprouting seeds is one of the easiest ways you can grow your own food. All you need is a few clean glass jars (200g coffee or large jam size), some muslin or old net or nylon curtain material, some elastic bands and a warm dark place, such as an airing cupboard.

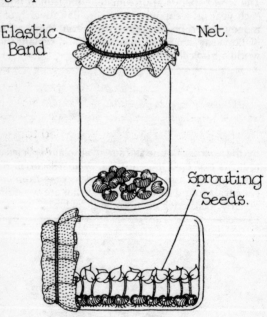

Elastic Band — Net.

Sprouting Seeds.

Sprouted seeds are great in salads and brilliant for stir-fry dishes. You can sprout many kinds of seeds. Your local health food store will have some in stock. The bean sprouts so popular in Chinese food are sprouted from mung beans. They are cheap to buy and easy to grow, so start with them. By having a number of jars on the go, starting a fresh one each day, you will have a constant supply ready to eat.

Experiment with small quantities first until you discover how much you will use. A handful of beans to each jar will do to start with. Wash the beans and soak them for twenty-four hours, then rinse and drain off all the water. Rinse the jar and put in the beans and fasten the net lid (see diagram). Put the jar in the airing cupboard or in another warm, dark place on its side, with the beans spread along the glass sides. The beans will need rinsing each day with clean water, which can be done through the lid without the need to remove it. This way the beans will not flush down the drain. When the shoots are about 2 to 4 cm long, they are ready to eat. Clean each jar and lid thoroughly after each harvest.

15

Don't send death down the drain. Make sure your home uses phosphate-free washing products and a water-softener to take out calcium and magnesium ions.

16

Sixty litres of water are needed to refine one litre of oil. We could save fifty million litres of oil each year if everyone cleaned and reused the sump oil from all our motor vehicles. Never pour oil of any kind down the drain. Check with your local authority for safe disposal.

17

If you buy something today, choose the item with the least packaging and don't let the shop put it in another bag. Use a shopping basket instead of a new carrier bag for each trip. Think about the environment every time you shop.

18

Around a hundred species of parrot, almost one in three of the earth's total, are in danger of becoming extinct. Loss of their natural habitat is their greatest threat, but trapping is also a real problem. If you want any kind of 'exotic' pet, make sure it has been bred in this country.

19

You can find the tallest flowering plants on earth in the forests of Western Tasmania, in Australia. The *eucalyptus regnans* is surely one of the wonders of the world, the tallest tree reaching 125 metres.

20

The best way to get from A to B in the kindest way possible to the environment and the most beneficial to you, is to WALK. It is pollution free, it is cheap, and it helps you keep fit.

21

There are eleven different kinds of grasshoppers in the British Isles. Each one has a different song. Only the males 'sing' — they are trying to attract a female. They rub their back legs against their wings to create the sound.

PURCHASE POWER

Every time you buy something you influence the planet's future. Not so long ago it was practically impossible to buy unleaded petrol in Britain. The existence of environmentally friendly alternatives to everyday household cleaning products, such as washing powder, was unthinkable. What changed? You did! As awareness of the planet's plight spread, the desire to do something about it increased. On an individual basis, the first thing we could do was clean up our act at home. We demanded safer alternatives, and the market was forced to respond.

By choosing the green option wherever possible, we will alter what goods are produced and how they are sold. Farming practices will change if we refuse to buy battery eggs, pesticide-riddled food and medicated meat. If all the goods sold in too much packaging and nonbiodegradable or nonreturnable containers, were left on the supermarket shelves, the stores would have to think again. If all the products which had been tested on animals ceased to sell, the manufacturers would close, just as most of the fur trade outlets have already done, or change their thinking.

Stop before you shop! Stop and think about what you are buying. Do you really need it? In the western world we all consume much more than we need — not just food, but all things. Make sure you know exactly what you are buying. Read the labels; where does it come from, what is it made of? Always buy the largest-size containers; this saves on packaging and shopping trips. You can be a real influence in steering your family along the green path. Educate yourself and them. Ask for green books for birthdays and Christmas, and learn as much as you can.

It is you and your age group who will inherit the earth and whatever mess goes along with it. Start now to protect your inheritance.

January

22

A slowworm looks like a snake. It is neither slow nor a worm or even a snake. It is in fact a legless lizard. Watch it blink; snakes don't have eyelids. It is a benefit to people, eating many garden 'pests'.

23

If you have permission to walk over farmland and need to go through a gate, don't forget to close it. If it is locked and you must climb it, always climb on the hinged side, which is stronger.

24

Access to water is vital for birds, not only for drinking. Daily bathing keeps feathers in tiptop condition — very important for insulation. Never add chemicals to a bird bath to stop it freezing in winter.

25

Hedgehog fleas do not like humans.

26

Just like adaptable humans, animals that can adapt to different enviroments easily seem to thrive the best in the 'civilized' world of the town. Rats, mice, foxes, gulls, crows, starlings and pigeons are just a few. Try and think of some more.

27

Always write on both sides of a piece of paper. Save scrap paper for note pads for shopping lists or telephone messages. Encourage adults to answer letters by replying on the same sheet of paper and tell them to explain why they do it.

28

In one January night, the once uncommon hurricane-force winds wiped out an ancient survivor. The village of Selborne lost its oldest resident, a fifteen-hundred-year-old yew tree.

29

Four to five million red-eared terrapins are bred each year to satisfy the pet trade. Most die within the first year due to ignorance of their needs in captivity. They are also captured in the wild for human consumption, mainly in the Far East and Western Europe.

30

Marine turtles have been leaving the sea to lay their eggs on sandy Mediterranean beaches for about 100 million years! Development for tourism is now a severe threat to many of these sites.

31

Over the last ten years around 264 million wild-flower bulbs have been uprooted in Turkey. These are illegally sold to European gardeners, with false labels of origin put on by unscrupulous dealers. Perfectly shaped bulbs are unlikely to be from wild stock.

TRADE IN TOOLS

The best thing we can possibly give starving people in the Third World countries is a means to help themselves. A little-known organization called Tools for Self Reliance is trying to do just that.

You can help them by organizing collections of unwanted tools in your area. If you are good with your hands, you could also be involved in the repair part of their work.

Door-to-door collecting is very time-consuming, and should never be done alone without an adult, so other methods are preferable. Put a card in a local shop window or on the supermarket small ads board offering to collect tools. Again, you should have an adult with you when you knock on strangers' doors. Advertise on the school notice board, and perhaps you could involve the wood and metalwork teachers. Ask a large DIY store if they will allow you to have a collection point there at the weekend.

Basic hand tools are what is required — the sort used in woodwork, metalwork and building. Gardening and agricultural tools are not needed.

There are fifty local groups nationwide, and to find out the location of your nearest one, telephone 0703 869697. The London workshop can be contacted on 071-284 1311.

February

1

Tigers normally attack their prey from behind. To protect themselves Indian workers wear face masks on the back of their heads when going into the forest. IT WORKS!

2

Only half the amount of energy it takes to make paper is needed to make recycled paper. And only 100,000 litres of water is used in the production of one tonne of recycled; three times that amount is needed to produce new paper.

3

Lichens only grow where the air is clean. They are extremely slow growers — a reasonable-size plant could easily be fifty years old. The long-tailed tit builds its nest with them; many moths use their patterns as camouflage.

4

Spot the difference. The coot is a black water bird with a white bill and white forehead. The moorhen is a black water bird with a red bill and white side stripes and under-tail feathers.

5

All the golden hamsters ever kept as pets are descended from thirteen found in the Middle East in 1930. Their average lifespan is three years and adults should not be caged together. At temperatures below 18°C they are likely to become sleepy.

6

Pigeons are famous for their homing abilities but salamanders are even better at using the earth's magnetic field to find their way home.

7

Water covers three-quarters of the world's surface. For many people it is the most precious commodity and the most difficult to obtain. Only one per cent of the earth's water is available for us to drink; the rest is either salty or frozen.

PLANTS TO LIVE WITH

When a friend put her house on the market, the estate agent told her to buy some large healthy house plants. He said that houses always sell quicker when they have lots of plants. Why don't you try and make your bedroom or other rooms more cheerful and friendly by growing some plants? Plants like spider plants, ivies and castor oil plants are easy to grow. I always find myself more at ease in houses with healthy plants. Plants do affect the home environment, just as on a large scale they are vital to the world.

You don't have to spend a fortune to have a house full of plants. Taking cuttings from friends' plants is extremely easy. The secret of keeping house plants healthy is to remember a few basic common-sense tips.

Don't over or under water them. More plants die from root rot, due to too much water, than from too little water.

Make sure you know the correct temperature and light requirements for each individual plant. Look them up in a book.

Feed the plants regularly in the growing season.

Don't position the plants in draughty places.

Don't allow your plants to become pot-bound, repot them when the roots show through the base.

Keep the leaves clean, and regularly mist-spray the plants which need humidity. Standing pots on a gravel-filled tray with water in the base, not reaching the pots, is also good for increasing humidity.

Try to collect rainwater for watering, especially if you live in a hard-water area. If this is not possible, use tap water which has been boiled and left to cool.

TIPS ON REPOTTING

For single plants, do not choose a pot which is a lot larger than the last one. It is usually best to plant groups in a large container but still in individual pots. This makes it easier to change and repot later.

Take plant out of pot and then put the old pot inside the new one.

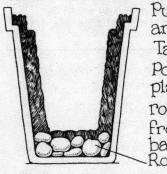

Put in compost and firm down. Take out old Pot. Put in plant with the roots released from compact ball.
Rocks for drainage.

February

8

Look out for kestrels if you travel on the motorways.
They have thrived, using the motorway verges as ideal
hunting grounds. Record the distance between
hovering birds, and you will have a good idea of how
big a territory each has. Males are smaller and more
colourful than females.

9

Over five million plastic containers are thrown into the
sea every day. Each year 22,000 tonnes of plastic
packaging and 136,000 tonnes of plastic fishing
equipment are dumped at sea.

10

Take a photograph of your garden today, then one
each month on the same day from the same spot. You
will be amazed at the differences you see in the
pictures. You do not notice much change on a day-to-
day basis.

11

Britain is still destroying six thousand kilometres of
hedgerows every year. As well as concentrating on
world environmental problems, we must also put our
own 'house' in order.

12

China has the largest population of any country in the world. There are over one thousand million people living there. People are expected to have only one child per family, and are not allowed to marry until the man is twenty-two and the woman is twenty years old.

13

Don't eat frogs' legs! Most of them are caught in India, about seventy million every year. Their legs are cut off while they are still alive. The insects the frogs would normally eat are then destroyed using DDT, banned here because of the dangerous side effects.

14

Is the loft in your house insulated? Massive amounts of energy are wasted through heat loss. Heat rises, so the best place to start on insulation is the roof. Why don't you offer to help this weekend?

FIT FOR THE WORLD

It is easy when you are young to think that you will always be healthy, that what you do now will not affect the future. The way we live influences the wellbeing of the world. If we use all the planet's resources today, what will we have left for tomorrow? It is exactly the same on a personal level. It is your responsibility to take care of yourself.

There are many obvious things you can do to help keep fit, and it is never too early to start. Taking regular exercise is a great habit to acquire. The key to regular exercise is fun! Do something you really like, such as dancing, swimming, skating, cycling, jogging or brisk walking.

Thinking about your diet is important. Junk food is often an easy alternative, always available, and quite often delicious. However, if you think about what you are eating, the temptation is a lot easier to resist. Hamburgers are loaded with fat, and they contain gristle, sinew, offal and additives. Chicken pieces are usually from birds who have had no chance of a natural life, fed on additive-laced food. The massive amount of waste in the packaging of fast food is enough to make you think twice. Animals do not have to die to keep us alive. There is no need for the human animal to eat meat to have a good healthy balanced diet.

Fresh fruit and vegetables are delicious, especially organically grown ones. Try to train your palette to choose the healthy versions and avoid sugar and too much coffee and tea.

Smoking is stupid. I know — I've done it. You don't realize how much you and your clothes stink if you smoke. Try kissing someone who smokes. It is a prop when you are uneasy in a public situation but it doesn't make you look better, just insecure and dumb. It is bad for you, so why do something that could shorten your life? If you start smoking it is difficult to stop. Don't add another problem to your life.

Drugs and alcohol are all on offer at some time in your life. You will have choices to make which can affect your health for ever. Be wise. You don't have to follow the crowd if they choose the wrong path.

It isn't always easy to do the thing you know is right, but by taking care of yourself you also take care of the planet. You are both worth it.

15

Fluorescent lights last much longer if you don't switch them on and off frequently.

16

Make your own potting compost from household and garden waste. Try not to buy peat; the peat bogs are rapidly declining from overharvesting. These bogs are unique wildlife habitats, thousands of years old.

17

The term 'dead as a dodo' is often used. The dodo is an example of people's ignorance in their dealings with wildlife. Ths trusting flightless bird was exterminated on Mauritius in 1662, only a relatively short time after it was discovered.

18

Not all piranha fish are the frenzied killers you see in films. There is a vegetarian variety in the Amazon which eats fruit; in doing so, it helps to spread the seeds, just as many birds do here.

19

A revolutionary new biodegradable plastic has been developed, made by bacteria which feed on sugar. Unlike conventional plastics, it really does breakdown leaving no pollution.

20

Britain only burns ten per cent of its waste. The rest is dumped in landfill sites, creating a 'time bomb' of problems for future generations.

21

Ten million homes in the United Kingdom have some kind of pet. Are you taking care of yours to the best of your ability? Read all you can about any pet before buying one.

HERBS FROM PLOT TO POT

Herbs are not just for flavouring cooking, they have been used by people and animals as medicine for thousands of years. Watch your dog eating grass when he has an upset stomach and needs to vomit. It has become fashionable again to drink herb teas and to use alternative medicine.

You don't need a huge area to grow herbs, in fact a window box or a tub will do. Most herbs can be dried but fresh ones are by far the best. Remember dried herbs are stronger, so you will need more when using fresh. Grow yours from seed as it is by far the cheapest method. If you are only growing a few plants, you could share some seed packets with friends.

If you are planning a window box, make sure you put the plants which require more water all at one end of the box. When you water the box you can raise up the end with the dry-loving plants. Put less drainage holes in the 'wet' end.

Herbs with small leaves, such as thyme and rosemary, will prefer much more sun and less water than their softer, lusher relatives such as mint and parsley. It is a good idea to find out which country the plants come from, to help you decide where to plant them.

There is little point in spending time and energy growing something you don't like. It is possible to buy fresh herbs in most areas, so taste them first.

There are lots of books in the library about the uses of herbs. If you are lucky you might also find some really cheap very old second-hand books full of 'old wives' tales' which sound like witches' spells. Aromatherapy relies on essential oils distilled from herbs such as lavender.

Pots of growing herbs or dried herbs in pretty jars make lovely gifts. You could even consider selling your produce as a fund-raising venture. Organic growing is essential, so you might be able to supply your local organic food store.

22

Despite all the extinctions, new animals are still being discovered. A black short-tailed tree-climbing kangaroo has recently been found in New Guinea.

23

Tortoises have been around for two hundred million years. In the last hundred years human beings have been responsible for the near extinction of several of the forty-five species.

24

If you have a tree in your garden, bury any leftover bones you have beneath it. They will rot down over the years, slowly supplying nutrients to the tree.

25

It is not only parrots and mynah birds that copy sounds they hear. Young male chaffinches learn their songs from their fathers. Many other birds do the same. Listen to your local dominant male starling; he copies lots of other birds.

26

If you have to travel by car, try and share the journey.
Organize your friends into a car pool for regular
journeys. In Los Angeles employers who don't
organize car sharing are fined!

27

Fishermen are now becoming so efficient that our
favourite British meal of fish and chips is likely to
disappear. Nearly two-thirds of all the cod and
haddock in the North Sea are caught each year,
leaving insufficient breeding stock.

28

New Zealand is home to one of the world's strangest
and rarest parrots. The kakapo is not only the largest
parrot but the only flightless and nocturnal one. There
are around forty left, and an intense programme for its
conservation is under way.

29

It seems that, like humans, most monkeys
are right-handed. However, most parrots
are left-footed.

FAST INSTEAD OF FAST FOOD

In the western world we all eat far more than we actually need to survive.

In the Third World the vast majority of the people have nowhere near sufficient food and many are starving. We cannot possibly know what it feels like, never to have enough to eat, every day seeing illness and death. What we can do is help the agencies who are working in these countries to help the people gain dignity and independence through their own efforts. The best way for us to help is to give money. With your parents' permission and assistance, why don't you work out how much one day's food would cost you, and do without it, giving the money saved to OXFAM or a similar charity.

Make sure that everyone is fit and healthy and try to involve your family and friends — as many people as possible. Restrict yourselves to water and four slices of bread, one for each meal. Plan your fast on a weekend when you can keep your activity to a minimum. Drink plenty of water and keep in mind throughout the day what it feels like, and why you are doing it.

March

1

Africa's black rhino population has drastically decreased in the last thirty years. Around only four per cent of the animals remain. Rhino horn is of no known medical use, but ignorant people buy it to make a 'love potion'.

2

The tuatara is an animal in a scientific classification of its own (*Sphenodon punctatus*). This reptile has not changed in more than eighty million years. It is a real living fossil!

3

Choosing 'organic food' is not only important for your health; most agrochemical fertilizers are produced from oil and coal, both nonrenewable resources.

4

Glow-worms and fireflies are in fact beetles. They use their 'glow' to attract a mate. Different species use their light in different ways, often sending flashes like Morse code.

5

Sulphur is the main cause of acid rain. Nearly all the sulphur in the skies of North America and Europe is made by people, the result of burning oil and coal.

6

Britain is the worst country in Europe for polluting the sea. We dump millions of tonnes of waste into the sea every year.

7

Each year the United Kingdom imports one and a half million doors made from tropical hardwoods. Nearly all of this wood comes from cutting down trees in forests with no replanting programmes. Don't buy toys made of tropical hardwoods – get pine or beech ones instead.

TRACKS AND TRAILS

Take a walk in the country or the park or along the river bank or the beach today and see how many different species of animals and birds you can spot. You do not necessarily have to 'see' each one, but you must be able to identify the signs which tell you it lives nearby.

Get a cassette of bird songs, and teach yourself which is which. Read as much as you can about the habits and habitat of birds and animals to enable you to understand them. Train your senses to spot the clues that will surely be all around you.

The tracks animals leave in soft mud, snow or sand can be very revealing. Take a sketch-pad and ruler with you and draw the tracks to scale. This will make identification much easier, when you visit the reference library. Photograph and make lists of everything you see which looks like the work of wildlife. Take samples of feathers, bones and half-eaten seeds – in fact, anything that will give a clue. Look out for a brilliant book by Hugh Falkus called *Nature Detective* published in 1978 by BCA. You should still be able to borrow it from the library.

Droppings are another sure sign of life, and their condition can show whether the animal was there recently or not. Note the position of droppings and anything else in the near vicinity. Signs of a recent kill should be closely examined as many animals eat the same prey but do it in different ways. A badger eats his kill on the spot but a fox will drag it away, leaving a telltale trail.

Make records of what you find and keep returning to the same area to monitor any changes. If the area you regularly patrol ever comes under threat, your records could be a vital weapon in the case for the defence.

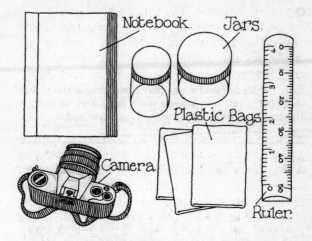

8

Shags, gannets and pelicans are all related. They are the only birds to have all four toes webbed.

9

Not only birds build nests in the breeding season; the stickleback, our best-known pond fish, does so too. The male builds a nest to attract his mate and vigorously defends his territory.

10

The honey bee was first brought to this country from Asia. Our ancestors soon discovered its use as a plant pollinator as well as a food producer. Drones, workers and one queen make up the colony. The queen can lay up to two thousands eggs per day in the summer.

11

The oldest known painting depicts three species of geese. The Egyptian tomb painting at Medum is from the early Fourth Dynasty, around 3000 BC.

12

In 1988 there were already twenty-six universities and one polytechnic in the UK offering courses on the environment and ecology.

13

A temperature of 1200°C is needed to incinerate PCBs (polychlorinated biphenyls) without producing highly toxic dioxins. These can cause birth defects in animals and humans.

14

Don't waste money on buying a 'poop scoop'. It is important to clean up after your dog, but use an old plastic carrier bag. Put your hand inside the bag to pick up the mess, then turn the bag inside out. Take it home and bin it.

WALLS HAVE EARS, IF YOU LET THEM!

Walls can be extremely important wildlife habitats if a little thought goes into their construction. A perfectly pointed brick wall is of little use to plants or animals, but once a suitable climbing plant is trained up it, then it does not take long for the creatures to follow.

Obviously there are restrictions on what you can do to the walls of the house, but the

Dry Stone Walls.

Cross Section.

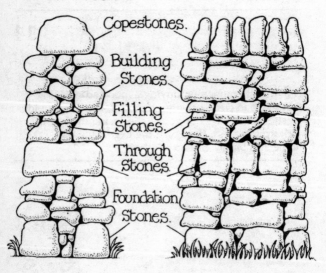

Copestones.

Building Stones.

Filling Stones.

Through Stones.

Foundation Stones.

garden is another story. If you are about to have a new wall in your garden, offer to help – and try to influence the design so that it is a good one for wildlife.

Dry-stone walling is quite a skill, and you will need a lot of patience and practice. It is worth doing if you can, because the unevenness and the gaps make ideal homes for all sorts of plants and animals. An old dry-stone waller from North Yorkshire told me that the secret of good walling was 'Once you pick up a stone, you find a place to put it in the wall, and you never put it down again.' All that takes a very skilled eye.

If you are having an ordinary wall made of evenly cut stone, you can still make it more acceptable to wildlife. Leave some gaps between the slabs, without mortar, and half-fill them with earth. You can plant alpine-type plants in these gaps. Bear in mind which way the wall is facing and choose light or shade-loving plants accordingly. Make sure the plants have adequate drainage. If it is quite a large wall then try to leave some larger gaps suitable for small mammals, reptiles or amphibians.

March

15

When you next go shopping for new clothes, look at the labels. Try and choose unbleached naturally dyed cotton. Twenty-five thousand barrels of oil are used each day in the making on nonbiodegradable synthetic fabrics.

16

The giant salamander is 180 centimetres long — the largest living amphibian. They live in mountain streams in China and Japan and are severely threatened by overhunting.

17

The two-toed sloth appears to be green at first sight. But if you looked more closely, you would see the algae which grow on its fur, a special form only growing on sloths. In return for its home it repays the sloth with camouflage.

18

Think about flower's names. Many of them have meanings. The daisy is so called because it closes its petals when night falls: 'Day's eye'. Night-scented stock only produces its perfume during the night.

19

The earth's central-heating system is maintained by the oceans' currents. Global warming can drastically alter these and our climate would be irreversibly changed. It has already started; the ice in Greenland is several degrees warmer than it was a few years ago.

20

The United States is home to the oldest known living tree. A bristlecone pine growing in the White Mountains is over four and a half thousand years old.

21

If we continue to use oil at our present rate of consumption, the existing supply will run out by the year 2035.

REUSE OR RECYCLE

Have a total rethink day. Try and look with fresh eyes at all the things your household uses every day. Start first thing in the morning and make a list; you'll be amazed at the results. Work out ways in which everyone can consume less. Try and make your home have the lightest rubbish bin in the street.

Find out what can go on the compost heap. Storage is always a problem when it comes to recycling. It is silly to waste energy travelling to a recycling facility too often with small amounts of materials. Sort out suitable storage sites today. A good strong cardboard box in a shed or garage or under the stairs is ideal for all your waste paper. You can then leave the box and its contents out for collection (if you are lucky enough to have collections in your area) or drop the whole thing into the recycling collection point. Remember to store paper safely, away from flammable substances.

As you will not be buying drinks in plastic bottles, you will probably have quite a lot of glass bottles as well as jam jars. Wherever possible, reuse the jars as they are easy to clean. Have a special bin for the rest of the glass, which should be sorted into colours and deposited in the bottle bank. Remember to remove the tops of the bottles and containers. Again, store them until you have a really good load. Try and get another couple of families involved and share the journeys.

Pure aluminium cans are excellent for

recycling. Check each one with a magnet to make sure it is pure aluminium. Try and get a can-saving project going at school.

Any old clothes can be used for numerous things. They can be unpicked and restyled, given to charity shops, cut up and used as cleaning cloths. Wool and cotton can be composted, and they can even make additional loft insulation.

Ask at your local council offices where your nearest recycling depots and bottle banks are, and ring Freephone 0800 444222 for aluminium can information.

March

22

All 'hardwoods' are not hard; balsa wood used so
often in model making, is a hardwood. The conifer
family of trees produces the so-called 'softwoods'; and
trees which bear flowers and are much slower to grow
produce the hardwood.

23

Crabs shed their outer skins as they grow; a new shell
hardens from underneath. Snails have the same shell
for life. It grows from the edge and thickens with age.

24

Polar bears have such efficient heat-insulating fur that
infra-red cameras, normally used to photograph warm-
blooded animals, do not detect them. An individual
hair is transparent and hollow; it appears white
through light reflection.

25

After it has hibernated, a toad will return to the same
pond each year to seek a mate. Some routes are
centuries old but are now across roads. In 1969
Switzerland was the first country to experiment with
toad tunnels under roads on the traditional migration
routes.

26

Male smooth newts grow a crest each year to attract a mate. They arrive at the breeding ponds a few weeks before the females. They have elaborate courtship displays and the females lay their eggs individually, unlike frogs and toads.

27

Chicken wire placed around a bush or over a hedge will prevent predators, such as magpies, squirrels and cats, from attacking birds' nests.

28

The Royal Society for the Protection of Birds has more than one hundred nature reserves in the British Isles.

29

Eighty per cent of wild birds caught for the pet trade will die before they reach the pet shop. Millions are imported into the EEC every year.

30

Each year half a million rattlesnakes are tortured and killed in Texas, USA. The 'rattler round-up' is a barbaric spectacle. It is also an ecological disaster because the snake's food animals are on the increase with potentially disastrous results.

31

Crocodiles are always cast in an unsympathetic light. Think of 'Crocodile Dundee' and the beast in 'Peter Pan'. In fact, only seven out of the twenty-two remaining species are dangerous. The animals themselves are practically the same as they were when they first appeared on earth 150 million years ago.

GARAGE SALE

The American idea of having a garage sale is becoming very popular in the UK. It is like a jumble sale, but you have it in your own garage. It is a chance to get rid of all the stuff that fills the attic, cellar, box room, shed and garage itself. If you haven't got a garage then the garden or street will do, but you are then more dependent on good weather. The stuff you sell should be all clearly price-labelled before you start. Collect the goods for a few weeks before the sale if you have somewhere to store them. People are usually very generous in both giving stuff and buying other stuff back, as long as it is for a good cause. Of course, you should have an adult with you for door-to-door collecting, and at the sale itself.

Make sure the sale is well publicized beforehand, with the name of your chosen charity clearly stated. When the sale is over you must make sure you get a written receipt from the charity for the amount you have raised. Keep the receipt and either display it in your window or make sure everyone knows it is available for inspection at any time.

If you have goods left at the end of the sale, either take them to a charity shop, if they are suitable, or arrange for them to be bought and collected as a job lot by a junk-shop owner. Don't expect a lot of money, but at least you won't be stuck with the stuff.

April

1

Chewing gum has resin from rainforest trees in it. The tree must be alive to harvest the resin regularly, so chewing gum might be helping to preserve some areas in Malaysia, Indonesia and the Amazon.

2

Buddhist scriptures have been preserved in Korea for seven centuries, on wooden tablets known as Tripitaka Koreana. There are more than 80,000 of them in the Haeinsa temple.

3

If you have large picture windows and you want to stop birds flying into them, fix a stick-on picture of a bird of prey, such as a sparrowhawk. These can be bought by mail order from the RSPB.

4

Frogs are early breeders, laying up to thirteen hundred eggs. They need to lay so many as only one in every fifty will leave the pond as a froglet. If your pond becomes overrun with frog spawn, contact your local naturalist group and they will help with relocation.

5

The rarest parrot in the world is the echo parakeet. It hails from Mauritius and there are no more than fifteen left. The Jersey Wildlife Preservation Trust is setting up a captive breeding programme on Mauritius, where it hopes to catch some of the remaining birds to breed under controlled conditions, and re-release when the time is right.

6

Colombia is the home of more bird species than anywhere else in the world. There are one thousand seven hundred different birds recorded breeding there.

7

In a dry spring remember the birds who build nests using mud. House Martins will greatly appreciate a home made muddy area, so soak a patch of soil regularly if there is no rain.

HELP A TOAD ACROSS THE ROAD

As the daylight hours lengthen and the temperature rises, our frogs and toads emerge from hibernation with only one thing on their minds. The race to reproduce is on. Frogs seem to be happy to deposit their eggs in any old puddle, but not the toads. They make long and often dangerous journeys to return to ponds they have known. Following invisible signs, they make their way by night.

As roads cut through almost every open stretch of countryside, the toad faces death on every journey. If you know of a 'toad road' in your area, you might be able to help. As the help is needed through the night, it is essential that you work with adults on this project. The Flora and Fauna Preservation Society has been involved in a nationwide campaign to assist local groups of toad helpers. Special road signs are put up at migration time to warn drivers.

Teams of helpers spend the nights collecting and counting the toads, before carrying them across the roads.

All you need is some light-coloured clothing and a few reflective stickers or armbands. You must be clearly visible to night drivers. A bucket will be useful and a notebook for toad data.

If you have any injured toads, the Wildlife Hospitals Trust will advise you on treatment. Telephone 0296 29860.

The first toad tunnel in the UK was constructed at Hambleden near Henley-on-Thames. In some places, ponds have been dug on the hibernation side of the road, to try persuading the toads to use them instead.

8

If you spot a pile of broken snails' shells on and around one particular stone, it is probably a song thrush 'anvil'. They often have a special stone for smashing open the shells of their favourite food.

9

Farming and forestry are the main causes of the stone curlew becoming one of Britain's rarest birds. This makes them an ideal target for egg collectors. Taking any bird's egg is illegal.

10

Use sheets of old cardboard to stop weeds growing in your vegetable garden. Cover the weeds between your crops with strips of cardboard; the lack of light will stop them growing. It is harmless and totally biodegradable.

11

If you go to the fair and see goldfish being used as prizes, do not have a go at the stall. Many goldfish die to provide these few surviving ones. Write to your local authority and complain; they issue the licence to the fair. Also tell the stall-holder why you are boycotting him or her.

12

A variety of habitats is vital to maintain our wildlife. Since 1955 half of the lowland fens in England have been drained. These unique areas are home to many creatures which are unable to adapt to life anywhere else.

13

The robber crab from the islands of the Indo-Pacific is a giant compared to its land-dwelling relatives. Its legs can be a metre across and it can weigh over three kilos.

14

The largest earthworm in the world comes from South Africa. It can reach seven metres long and three centimetres in diametre. Overgrazing and the lowering of the water table is putting it in danger of extinction. Worms play a vital role in soil condition.

SOW SOME SEEDS OF SUCCESS

There is great satisfaction to be had from growing things. You don't need loads of money or a huge garden, just a couple of seed trays and a few pots, some compost and some seeds. If you get to know someone with a large, well-kept garden, you probabaly won't even have to buy seeds, as they will give you some from their plants.

Whichever type of seed you choose, find out the best time to sow it. Spread your work over a period around that time so that you don't have all the plants ready at once.

Don't skimp on the compost but buy the best you can afford or – even better – use your own home made stuff. Don't buy peat, the pear moors are under severe threat. Make sure that the seed trays are absolutely clean to avoid problems with disease. Water the compost-filled trays before you sow your seeds, sow sparingly and then sift a fine covering of compost on to the seeds. Follow the seed packet instructions for temperature requirements of your particular crop.

When the seedlings are ready to 'prick out' (that means when they have sprouted and need separating so they have room to grow), prepare your pots. They must also be scrupulously clean. Put some clean rough gravel or broken pot into the base to assist drainage and fill up with new compost. Never use potting compost twice, again to prevent disease. Give the old compost to someone else, to spread on their garden, if you haven't got a garden. Again, water before putting your seedlings in, and remember how delicate young plants are.

Never handle the stems or roots. Always hold seedlings by a leaf. Remember to allow space for it to grow. Water the plant gently when its earth feels dry and allow the plants as much light as possible. Plants with a long stem and few leaves are suffering from lack of good all-round light. If you haven't got a greenhouse and are relying on the windowsill, then a light box is worth making. This simple device gives maximum light and encourages sturdy growth.

Strong Cardboard Box.
Inside lined with aluminium foil, shiny side out.

Leave a 5cm lip.

Base lined with one piece of foil to avoid watering problems.

15

One of the first known conservationists was
Jambeshwar. In the fifteenth century he founded the
Bishnois sect in Rajasthan in India. He wanted to
teach people to care for the environment.

16

In 1954 the animal disease myxomatosis arrived in
Britain. Rabbits died in their thousands; in some
places they were almost exterminated. Farmers
welcomed this but many other plants and animals
suffered irreversible damage as well. Stoats and
buzzards, whose main food is rabbit, disappeared
from some areas.

17

The last seven wild Arabian oryx were killed by
hunters in October 1972. Conservationists had noticed
its rapid decline and captive breeding stocks had been
established. After many years' work they were
reintroduced to the world, and ten years after the last
wild one died, the first wild-born baby arrived.

18

A new puppy must be frequently handled every day.
Get him used to having his ears, eyes and paws
checked regularly. This will make treating him for
future problems so much easier.

HIDE AND SEE

Without doubt the best way to observe animal behaviour is to get as close to your subject as possible. The animals must behave totally naturally for you to learn anything worthwhile about them. The secret is to see but not be seen. In other words, hide.

You can make a simple hide from camouflage material from an army surplus store. With a few bamboo poles and a bit of help, make a 'wigwam' which can be easily carried from location to location. Make a wigwam by cutting four big triangles, about seven feet high and three feet wide at the base. Sew all the sides together so that the points meet at the top, then join the final sides together, so that the material makes a pyramid shape when it is held up using four bamboo canes. Leave a slit in the final side to get in and out of and to watch through. There is no set fabric size, it depends on how big you want to make it. The material should be bought already proofed. Don't use polythene for waterproofing as it makes too much noise. String loops attached at intervals on the inside of the fabric will hold the poles in place.

However, the best hides are more permanent. If the structure is in place all the time, the animals and birds accept it as part of the territory.

If you haven't got access to a garden, then perhaps you could ask if you can build a hide on school land, or check with your local authority to see if they can suggest somewhere. A friendly farmer would be a real help.

You can salvage materials to construct your hide. Old doors or other wooden sheets are a good basis. Glass is dangerous and you shouldn't use it. Tin sheeting is not a good idea either. In summer it can make the hide extremely hot and in winter it can be freezing. Again, you will need adult help with this project.

Remember to put the entrance in the side furthest away from your proposed observation site. Make viewing slots large enough to see a reasonable area. Waterproofing is very important if you intend to use the hide in all weathers. However fascinated you are with animal behaviour, sitting soaking wet can rapidly dull your enthusiasm.

Natural plant cover is the best for permanent hides, but until your cover grows you can paint it. Use environmentally safe paint in suitable camouflage colours.

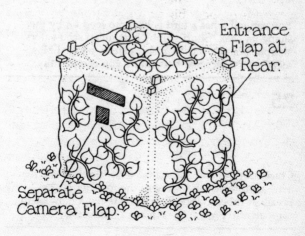

Entrance Flap at Rear.

Separate Camera Flap.

April

22

Rodents' teeth grow all the time. If you keep a pet hampster, mouse, rat, gerbil, guinea pig or chinchilla, remember they need to gnaw on wood and other substances regularly.

23

Quinine found in tonic water and used in medicine comes from the chinchona tree found in the tropical rainforests of Amazonia. Native peoples recognized its worth and western scientists developed its use in the treatment of malaria.

24

You can tell what a bird is likely to feed on by the shape its beak. Short stubby bills mean seed eaters, sharper pointed bills — insect eaters, hooked bills — meat eaters, etc. See how many you can identify.

25

Chico Mendes was assassinated by hired killers in 1988 aged forty-four. He was the founder of the Brazilian rubber tappers' union. He led a nonviolent campaign to protect the Amazon rainforests.

26

You need a licence to photograph a barn owl at its nest. This beautiful bird has suffered severely from changing farming practices and loss of suitable nesting sites.

27

In the dry northern outback of Australia, the termite hills are an amazing sight. They are flat-sided constructions up to six metres high, housing as many as two million termites.

28

Penguins are only found in the Southern Hemisphere. There are seventeen different species. They can 'fly' through the water using their wings like flippers, at over 25 m.p.h.

29

Fruit flies are often used in scientific research because they have 'giant' chromosomes, making it easy to study their genetic codes and work out hereditary features.

30

One of the first underwater observers was Alexander the Great. He used a glass diving bell to look at creatures below the surface of the Aegean Sea in 322 BC.

HAVE FUN TODAY:
Do whatever makes you laugh long and loud

When we laugh, our bodies release chemicals which actually make us feel good.

Spend time with people you love and who love you.

Stroke dogs and cats.

Hug someone you know. Touch is one of our most underrated senses. You must have noticed on wildlife films how much physical contact occurs between animals who live in groups. We are animals and we need it too. It has almost disappeared from our so-called civilized societies, which is a great pity.

T ender
O verwhelming
U nderrated
C aring
H ealing

IT IS NOT SOPPY OR STUPID OR WIMPY. IT'S – WONDERFUL! ! ! ! ! ! ! !

May

1

LD50 is a test carried out to measure how poisonous a product is. It is carried out on many household consumer products. Rats or mice are force-fed on the product until half of them die. All kinds of beauty and household goods are tested in this way. Make sure you buy cruelty-free products.

2

If you haven't got a garden but fancy growing things; why not volunteer to do the gardening for an elderly neighbour and divide the produce?

3

Trying to choose a birthday present for someone? You could buy them a year-long gift of a subscription to a conservation organization.

4

Butterflies have the ability to see ultraviolet as well as the colours we see. Caterpillars use camouflage for defence, often mimicking their host plants. Some store poisons from their food and warn their predators of the danger by their bright-coloured markings.

5

Cuckoos lay eggs with a matching pattern to the host bird's own. They lay them in around twenty seconds as opposed to the normal time for other birds of twenty minutes.

6

Isn't it incredible, even after very severe winds some birds' nests still remain in the trees, when brick and concrete buildings crumble?

7

The tomatoes you grow are easy to keep and cultivate because they incorporate several genes of their wild relatives from South America.

CLOCHES

This is a cheap and easy way to encourage your garden plants to grow early. By keeping the ground just a few degress warmer, you get an earlier crop. It is possible to buy purpose-made cloches of various shapes and sizes, but in the spirit of *Greendays* it is much better to make your own, recycling material already available.

A visit to the greengrocer will provide you with frames for larger cloches. The leaf-vegetable crates made from rough-cut wooden slats are ideal. These crates are thrown away, so the shopkeeper should be happy for you to remove them. Many of these vegetable crates have widely spaced slats which let in lots of light but if all you can find are ones with the boards nailed closely together then ask an adult to pull away every other board so you are left with just enough to hold the frame together. This will let in all the light your plants need. The damaged crates not suitable for cloches will make firewood. The thinly cut wood is ideal as tinder with twisted sheets of old newspaper. Kept dry, it lights very quickly. Don't try it for yourself, though. Save it for family fires.

For cloches which will cover a row of seedlings, wire coat hangers make ideal frames. You will need to cover your frames, whether wood or wire, with clear polythene. So much of this is thrown away it should be quite easy to get hold of all you need. Try a furniture store or any other shop selling large items. These goods invariably arrive in huge poly bags, which are disposed of when the items are displayed. Or wait till your parents get something back from the dry cleaners – they always put clothes in polythene.

Individual plant-pot cloches can be as simple as a polythene bag. They can also be made from half a plastic drinks bottle. Use the end with the top so you can adjust the air and water supply without removing the cloche, and so losing heat.

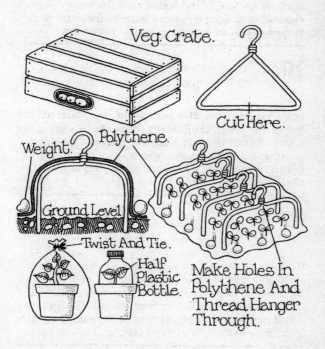

Veg. Crate.

Cut Here.

Weight. Polythene.

Ground Level.

Twist And Tie.

Half Plastic Bottle.

Make Holes In Polythene And Thread Hanger Through.

8

Don't be photographed with 'tame' baby wild animals when you are on holiday. They are drugged and suffer appalling cruelty. When they are caught in the wild, their parents are killed, and they are smuggled out, then killed off when they are too old to be cute.

9

Jamaica has more native plants and animals than any other Caribbean island. Around a thousand different ones are known. Island habitats are the most vulnerable to devastion from 'natural disasters'. With limited space, the wildlife is unable to recover.

10

Not all sharks are killers such as the one portrayed in the movie 'Jaws'. The basking shark can be seen in the waters around the British Isles. It prefers the warmer months, when it comes to feed on plankton. Reaching fifteen metres long, it is an impressive sight, but totally harmless.

11

Catalytic converters are to be fitted as standard to some cars sold in Britain from 1990. If a new family car is likely, bear this in mind. A car with a catalytic converter reduces pollution from the exhaust. Even so, it still produces a lot of carbon dioxide, adding to the 'greenhouse effect', so it's still better to walk or cycle.

12

Make sure the peanuts you feed to wild birds are safe.
Many birds die from eating nuts containing high levels
of aflatoxin. Look for the Bird-food Standards
Association's 'seal of approval' on your next purchase.

13

Just like us, butterflies need the sunshine. They must
bask in it until their flight muscles have reached a
temperature of 30° C or they are unable to fly.
Buddleia and michaelmas daisies attract them, so
persuade your parents to plant either of these.

14

Leave a patch of nettles in your garden. You may not
like them, but the tortoiseshell, red admiral and
peacock butterflies all love to feed on them.

PONDER NO LONGER:
Do it in the spring, make a pond

A pond is the single most important contribution you can make, on a personal level, to wildlife conservation. A good healthy pond can harbour a great variety of plant and animal life. If you haven't got a garden, ask if you can make one for someone else.

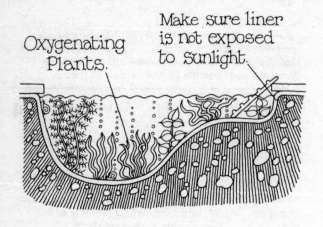

Oxygenating Plants.

Make sure liner is not exposed to sunlight.

Using pond lining and making your own design is harder work for you and your family, but you will have your own unique bit of habitat. You will need to decide your pond size and choose the type of liner. Take advice from your local garden centre.

Quantity of liner required:

DEPTH OF POOL × 2 + LENGTH OF POOL
= LENGTH OF LINER NEEDED

DEPTH OF POOL × 2 + WIDTH OF POOL
= WIDTH OF LINER NEEDED

Line the hole with lots of old newspapers to prevent the lining tearing when the water is added. Remember water is extremely heavy, so there will be a lot of pressure on the lining.

Some water from an established pond will help to get yours colonized quickly. Do not keep goldfish if you want a proper wildlife pond; introduce some sticklebacks instead. Start with lots of plants that will produce oxygen, such as Elodea Densa (available from garden centres) which will keep water healthy for animals and fish. Thin plants out as they grow, otherwise the algae will take over.

Whichever sort of pond you choose, remember to have one shallow end with some sort of ramp, made out of wood or wire, to allow any animals that have fallen in to escape.

The larger the pond the better, but avoid putting it in a very shady area, and keep it away from trees as falling leaves are a real problem. Another extremely important factor is safety. If there are any young children in the family, a child-proof fence of some kind must be used until they grow older.

Fibreglass ready-made ponds are easy to use. As long as you make a hole bigger than the pond and fill the gaps with lots of sand, all should be well. The only problem is that you are stuck with a rigid shape.

May

15

Chlorofluorocarbons or CFCs are damaging the ozone layer. They are used in foam packaging, aerosols, refrigerators and the more modern 'cooler' dry cleaning machines.

16

Caddis flies, mayflies and dragonflies all start their lives as underwater creatures.

17

You can grow your own tomatoes on a balcony with good healthy results if you use organic growbags. Ask at your garden centre.

18

Britain has about three hundred thousand hectares of ancient woodland left. The Nature Conservancy Council (NCC) say that by the year 2025 the only bits we will have left will be in protected areas such as nature reserves.

19

Britain throws away around 23 million tonnes of waste every year. Much of this could be recycled. Think before you bin it!

20

Nuclear power produces less than four per cent of the energy we consume in Britain. The after-effects of this production will be with us for 250,000 years.

21

If you or your parents are about to buy a new electrical item, don't forget to check how energy-efficient it is. Even if it is slightly more expensive than its less efficient counterpart, buy it. You will save money in the end with lower bills, and you'll be helping to save the planet.

GROW A GREETING

You can make the most unusual card anyone has ever received, with a little forward planning. All you need is a couple of large pieces of cardboard, one corrugated, some polythene sheeting (taken from packaging), a piece of rough fabric such as an old dishcloth and a packet of mustard and cress seeds. You can also use some watercolour paints to add the finishing touches.

Decide on the greeting — it could be for a birthday or for Mother's Day or a Valentine — and pencil it on to the smooth side of the corrugated cardboard. If it is a long message then decide which bits to make the growing part. The rest can be written.

Make the lines of each letter about one centimetre wide, and cut out the words.

Make a tray exactly the same size as the corrugated card and about two centimetres deep with the plain rigid cardboard, painted to suit the greeting, and line it with the polythene. Then cut the fabric to fit exactly in the base. Make sure the fabric is damp, and then lay the corrugated card on top, smooth side up. Put some weights on each corner to keep it in position. Now sow the seeds through the cut-out areas. Remember to water regularly and turn the tray to prevent the plants leaning towards the light. The growth rate will depend on heat, light and water, so experiment before you make your first greeting.

When the seedlings are grown enough to spell your message clearly, allow the top of the corrugated card to dry and add any additional touches to the surrounding card with water colours. Remove the weights.

Deliver immediately.

Cross Section.

Weights.

Corrugated Card.

Polythene. Rigid Card. Rough Fabric.

Top View.

Optional Ribbon Around Edges.

HAPPY
MOTHERS
DAY
LOVE LISAxx

Seedlings.

22

Make sure all the eggs consumed in your house are
laid by free-range hens. Buy them in cardboard boxes
and take the box back to the shop for your next lot of
eggs.

23

EXTINCTION IS FOREVER. It is likely that in the last
thirty minutes another plant or animal has
disappeared from the face of the earth.

24

Ospreys returned to Speyside to nest in the 1950s. The
RSPB has been protecting their nest sites at Loch
Garten since 1959. By 1987, the Scottish population
had reached fifty pairs.

25

A code of conduct worth repeating: leave nothing but
footprints, shoot nothing but photographs, and only
take your memories.

26

The now extremely common grey squirrel was only introduced into this country around the end of the nineteenth century.

27

If you are transplanting seedlings, never handle the stem or roots. Hold them by the leaves. Give them lots of light to avoid spindly growth.

28

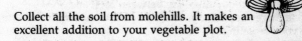

Collect all the soil from molehills. It makes an excellent addition to your vegetable plot.

29

The family cat can be a killer. Our feline pets kill
millions of birds every year. Fit a loud bell to your
pet's collar to avoid more dead 'presents' from him.

30

Bring home the groceries from the supermarket in a
cardboard box, then recycle it. If you must use plastic
carriers, use the same ones lots of times until they
wear out.

31

In Britain today there are between 3500 and 3800
additives used in our food. Do you know exactly what
you are eating?

CHECKLIST

Wherever you live you are surrounded by wildlife – in the heart of a city, in a high rise block of flats or in the depths of the country-side.

Spend today making a list of every living creature you see. Compare your list with your friends, and you'll be amazed at how many different living things you spot.

Insects, birds, animals should all be included. You could have a separate day for a plant check list. Decide how big an area you are going to check by marking it off on a street map or make a map of the area yourself. Give each part of the area a code number and then write this number down alongside a sighting of a creature. This way you will be able to tell exactly where you saw each animal. Don't forget the very small insects and remember to check your own home – it's not only outside that you get wildlife.

You can survey the same area at different times of the year and compare the difference.

June

1

Keep the leaves on house plants clean by using warm water and a soft cloth. Clean leaves aid photosynthesis, keeping the plant healthy. Spray them with a fine mist regularly.

2

The blue whale is the world's largest animal. It can weigh two hundred tonnes and be up to thirty metres long. It has been around for fifty million years, and is now in severe danger of becoming extinct, due to hunting.

3

By this time tomorrow another seventy-four thousand acres of tropical rainforest will have been destroyed.

4

The 'cartoon' cactus, traditionally associated with western movies is a target for poachers. Even the large plants are uprooted and sold illegally. The saguaro cactus can be one hundred and fifty years old.

5

In summer put out a very shallow brightly coloured dish of sugar water to attract butterflies. Try different-coloured dishes and see which one they prefer. They will also feed on rotting fruit.

6

If you see a ladybird, count its spots and see how many different spot and colour combinations you can find. Don't forget the yellow variety.

7

The adder or viper is our only venomous snake. The female is larger than the male and is a more sandy colour. It is not dangerous as long as it is left in peace. More people die from bee stings than adder bites but they are dangerous so avoid disturbing them.

NATURAL CLEANING

Check out your kitchen and bathroom cupboards and see how many different cleaning products there are. Most of these products are dangerous to the environment, detergents and bleaches pollute our rivers and seas and even ozone-friendly aerosols aren't good for the atmosphere. We do not need so many different liquids or powders to do these jobs. We can now buy many environmentally-friendly alternatives but there are also many old fashioned methods we can use. These use natural products, which do not kill if flushed down the drain, and are cheap and harmless. Try to revolutionize the way your family cleans in your household by returning to the natural and old fashioned ways. Here are a few tips – you can find out more for yourself from books of 'Household Hints'.

Use diluted hydrogen peroxide instead of household bleach. All that remains after natural breakdown is water and oxygen.

If you're out shopping with your parents, get them to buy vegetable-based detergents which are made from coconut or palm oils. These are completely biodegradable and the plants are a renewable resource.

Rings around the plughole in the bath or sink can be cleaned by sprinkling them with seasalt and then scrubbing them with half a lemon.

Keep a jar by the side of your basin and collect all those little slivers of soap that get discarded when you start a new bar. Pour boiling water over them and use the soft soapy mixture for hand-washing clothes.

Bicarbonate of soda makes a safe, natural scourer which you can use to scrub kettles, and clean stoves and sinks.

You don't need to buy floor cleaner — ordinary washing soda dissolved in hot water does just as good a job.

June

8

Fish gasping on the surface of a pond or aquarium means a lack of oxygen in the water. Increase the water flow with a pump and add more oxygenating plants. Make sure fish tanks are kept clean by filtering and regularly syphoning the debris from the bottom.

9

Satellite observations have recorded up to eight thousand separate fires in one day, in the forests of Brazil. All started by humans, of course.

10

If you don't approve of fur being worn by anything other than the animal born with it, contact LYNX, PO Box 509, Dunmow, Essex CM6 1UH, or phone 0371 872016. Offer your support in their campaign to make Britain fur-free.

11

Think twice before visiting a bullfight during a Spanish holiday. Your entry fee is supporting the event, even if it is only once.

12

Leaf vegetables should be cut into large pieces only just before cooking. Cut leaves exposed to the air lose more vitamin C.

13

Twenty per cent of the world's population is undernourished.

14

If you find a dead bird with a ring on its leg, make a note of the place and time and any other relevant facts relating to the death. Send the information and the ring to the British Trust for Ornithology (BTO), Beech Grove, Station Road, Tring, Hertfordshire HP23 5NR. If it is a bird of prey, phone for instructions: 044 282 3461.

INTERNATIONAL GREEN FRIENDS

It isn't possible for us all to travel around the world and see the different countries and their plants and animals. However, we can communicate with people all over the world. We regularly see news bulletins on our televisions but they invariably cover a lot of bad news and very little about the day-to-day lives of the ordinary citizens.

There are a number of worldwide conservation groups now, and they all send newsletters to their supporters. If you are a member of such an organization (and if not, why not?) then write to them, asking to be put in touch with members in the rest of the world.

The next time you send them proceeds of a fund-raising event you have organized, enclose a letter with some information about yourself – your age, hobbies and general interests – and ask if they can find some space to publish your request for contacts. Be patient as the newsletters are usually printed quarterly and it could be some time before you get any response. They also may not have space to print your letter for a while.

When you do start to get replies, please make sure you respond to everyone who takes the trouble to write to you. Don't forget to keep all the foreign stamps for fund-raising. Ask some of your friends with similar hobbies if they would like to write to people, and send their addresses to the people you will not be writing to on a regular basis.

Remember, whenever you are in contact with someone from another country, you are an ambassador for your own. Fortunately for us there are many countries in the world where the people speak English and so we don't have to do any work to communicate. Have you noticed it seems wherever a British TV crew is filming, they can always find a local person to give an interview in English? It must be so much more difficult for foreign crews trying to find British people to give interviews in other languages. As a nation we are so lazy when it comes to language learning. Making an attempt to learn another language can be fun and it will greatly improve your relations with people of other countries. Don't be put off languages if your only experience has been extremely boring classes at school. Some schools are forward-thinking enough to make languages fun, remembering that the first use of a language is to make yourself understood. Have you ever seen an English tourist abroad shouting in English to make the 'foreigners' understand? How much nicer it is to see someone attempting to speak the local language; notice how much more help they receive.

Find out as much as you can about your friend's life and environment. Who knows, you may be visiting them in person one day.

15

Collect clean used magazines and comics and check with local hospitals, doctors and dentists to see if they can use them.

16

Never use a metal file on your nails. Always use an emery board and file in one direction only. If you have white spots on your nails, check your calcium intake is sufficient.

17

Don't leave the TV and video on standby. Switch them off when you are not using them. It saves energy and is also safer.

18

Helping with the decorating? Wallpaper is an added insulation, so don't strip the old one before you apply the new.

19

If your parents are planting a holly bush to attract the birds, ask at the garden centre to make sure it is a female plant, as they bear the berries. You will need to have a male plant not too far away.

20

Have a sunflower-growing competition with your friends and leave the seeding heads for the birds to help themselves.

21

The last bullfight in England was held at the Agricultural Hall in Islington, north London, in March 1870. It was stopped by the RSPCA secretary John Colam, and Superintendent Green. The Spanish promoters were fined.

BARK RUBBING

This is a great way to learn about your local trees. You are probably quite familiar with brass rubbings, usually made in old churches. Bark rubbing is exactly the same technique, but is done on trees.

After the hurricane-type storms of recent years, many old trees are lying on the ground — making access to the trunks a lot easier. When a tree has a very rough bark, it is easier to make a rubbing if its trunk is large and the surface is not too curved.

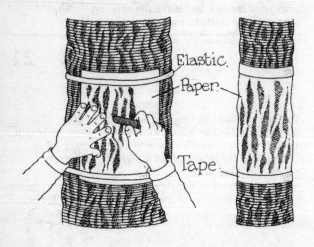

You need very little equipment to make rubbings. You can buy crayons from an art shop. Try to use fairly heavy recycled paper for the rough trees and lighter paper for the smoother ones. A large roll of thick elastic, a roll of wide sticky tape, a few bags and a pocket guide to trees are the other essentials.

Use the elastic to secure your paper to rough trees and the tape for the smoother ones. Never pierce the trunks with pins or nails. It can damage the tree and the paper always tears as soon as you start to rub. Rub gently over the whole area of the paper with the crayon, which will pick up the pattern of the bark. Try to keep the rubbing pressure even and cover a larger area than you need, so you can cut out the best bit for framing.

Some of the most attractive pictures I have ever seen were hung in a friend's hallway. They were made up of bark rubbings and pressed leaves.

Collect leaves, flowers and fruit at different times of the year, press them and assemble them with the bark rubbing. To complete the total presentation you could make the frame from the same kind of wood as the tree, and try to find out the history of the tree and how old it is.

June

22

Make sure in your kitchen you always keep fruit and vegetables in a cool dark place. They stay fresher that way.

23

Laurel, hemlock, ragwort, monkshood and bracken should be removed from animal pasture, as they are known to be poisonous.

24

Don't buy or make bird boxes or tables using wood with the bark left on. Once it dries out and the bark peels away, the joints will be unstable. Parasites can also hide in the nooks and crannies, and be a nuisance to the birds, and the boxes also won't be as waterproof as a smooth wood one.

25

When choosing wood for any kind of building, check the *Good Wood Guide*, published by Friends of the Earth.

26

The aloe plant is a living medicine. If you have a minor burn or scald or sunburn, break a leaf from the plant and squeeze the juice from it on to the affected area.

27

If your trainers smell, try sprinkling some bicarbonate of soda in them and leave it in overnight. Make sure you tip it all out when you next use them.

28

Madagascar has a unique collection of animals and plants. It is the world's fourth largest island at over one thousand six hundred kilometres long. The Madagascar periwinkle is used to make medicine for people with leukaemia.

29

A law still exists which says that a canary must be carried by an underground emergency team working in a coal mine.

30

Do not buy a plastic 'hamster ball' for your pet. Unlike when he's in a wheel, with a ball the hamster cannot decide for himself when he has had enough exercise.

GREEN (NOT POLITICAL) PARTY

If you are organizing a party for a birthday or just for fun, you can make it green and fun.

Send the invitations on recycled paper.

Dress styles could reflect the theme, e.g. they could be entirely second hand from a charity shop.

Fancy dress as animals or plants, or environmental disasters, or litter bugs, or alternative energies. I'm sure you can think of loads more.

Make the party food vegetarian and organic. Be adventurous and show how delicious this food can be. (The Vegetarian Society has some great recipes.)

Ask people to travel to the party in the most environmentally friendly way possible in their circumstances.

Do not use disposable glasses, cups, plates, cutlery or napkins.

If you have any kind of party games, base them on conservation, such as a quiz, or a treasure hunt in the garden, spotting green things.

Decorate the room to look like a rainforest.

Use your imagination.

ENJOY IT!

July

1

3,480,252 licensed scientific procedures – what we would call experiments – were carried out on live animals in the UK in 1988.

2

If you must use batteries, look out for the clear-cased solar-powered rechargeable ones. The other sort take fifty times as much energy to make as they give out!

3

When growing herbs, cut off the flowering buds. It is the leaves which you will use, so let the plant use all its energy for leaf production.

4

Is the water coming out of your hot tap too hot to put your hands in? Suggest turning the heater thermostat down, to save energy and money.

5

Remember plants in clay pots dry out much quicker than those in plastic one. Water them more frequently in hot weather or in centrally heated rooms.

6

Four pieces of fruit a day can help lower the cholesterol level in your blood, to give you a healthier heart for all your life.

7

Saltwater fish drink much more than freshwater fish, they lose their body fluids to the saltier water in which they live.

WALK ON THE WILD SIDE

Have you got a garden with a corner which your family will agree you can give over to wild flowers?

The bit of the garden with the most useless soil is the bit that will make the best wild-flower meadow. Think of the places where you have seen profusions of colour. These are quite often bits of scrub land or railway sidings. Do not expect to have an area teeming with flowers in the first year after sowing; they need a year to get established. Cut the area at least twice in the first summer to make the plants thicken out.

Wild-flower meadow-seed mixes are commercially available, but make sure they don't include the clover family of plants. All the plants in this group are so successful they tend to drown out the others. Mix the tiny seeds with silver sand before sowing, then you can easily see how much ground you have covered. Sow sparingly, each seed needs some space to develop. Unlike seeds in trays, these will not need thinning out.

In the second year you should see the fruits

of your labour. The flowers will attract all kinds of insects, who in return will attract the birds and mammals. At the end of July you should cut back the whole area. Keep the flowers for pressing. You will then have another flourish which should be cut at the end of September.

If you decide to add more varieties of flowers later on, remember you will need to grow them in pots first. They can then be planted out in the spring.

July

8

Eggs marked as 'farm fresh' are not the same as free-range. Farm fresh eggs are often produced by hens condemned to lives of unspeakable misery, confined to battery cages.

9

If we cannot halt the greenhouse effect, the habitats we are saving now may be of little use to the animals living there. They could alter drastically as the climate changes.

10

The Society for the Prevention of Cruelty to Animals was given the 'Royal' prefix by Queen Victoria in 1840. The RSPCA now has 208 branches in England and Wales.

11

In 1988 over six thousand experiments were carried out in UK laboratories on nonhuman primates (that means animals like apes or chimps). According to the RSPCA many of these extremely intelligent animals are wild caught. They are often kept in totally unsuitable cages.

12

Your body has to last you the rest of your life. Treat it well.

13

Use a fountain pen, the sort which you refill from a bottle of ink, rather than throwaway ballpoints.

14

Rosehip tea is a great source of vitamin C. Camomile tea has a very calming effect — a good bedtime drink.

ADOPT AN AREA

The cleaner, tidier and more well-cared-for an area looks, the better it is likely to stay. Most litter louts are more likely to drop litter in an area which is already polluted.

Choose somewhere which you know well and regularly visit with friends, and make it your group's responsibility. Advise your local authority that you are going to keep 'your' area tidy and ask them for extra litter bins, if there are not enough, and check that they are emptied often. Make posters showing what you are doing and ask the local shops to display them.

Try and involve as many people as possible, at school or in youth clubs. Encourage others to adopt their own areas. You could even have competitions to see who has the best-kept area.

When collecting litter, always wear gloves. You could keep the aluminium cans and glass bottles for recycling, if you can find a local storage place, until you have a large enough quantity to make a journey worthwhile. Check on all the recycling possibilities.

Remember to break open the plastic rings which hold drink cans together, before putting them in the rubbish. They are lethal traps to small mammals and birds, who get their heads stuck in the rings and eventually choke to death. Crush flat any cans which you are not recycling, as these are also potential death traps for small animals.

Take old plastic carriers with you to deal with dog dirt. Put your gloved hand inside the bag, collect the mess, and then turn the bag inside out over the mess, knot the top of the carrier and then bin it.

By your good example you will educate others.

Freephone
Aluminium Can Recycling Association
for nearest collection point: 0800 444222

15

If you live near the beach or you visit one on holiday, find out from the local environmental group if they organize any activities there. Surveys, monitoring, or just regular tidying sessions would be a good way to get involved.

16

Have you wasted any paper today? Up to seventeen trees are used to make one tonne of paper.

17

Dragonflies are beautiful and fast, being some of the speediest insects. The dragonfly nymph bears little resemblance to the flying beauty. Send SAE for more information to the British Dragonfly Society, 1 Haydn Avenue, Purley, Surrey   CR2 4AG.

18

Look out for books illustrated by Charles Tunnicliffe. He died in 1979 and left a legacy of superb wildlife studies. His accuracy was incredible, and his work is both beautiful and educational.

19

The elephant seal is the largest seal in the world, with adult males weighing over seven tonnes. They weigh fifty kilos at birth.

20

For one hundred years until 1960, wild cockatiels were caught in Australia and exported for the pet trade.

21

Sunlight takes 8.3 minutes to reach the earth.

BUTTERFLIES WELCOME

Butterflies always lift my spirits. They mean warm summer days and outdoor activity. With modern agriculture destroying many of our wild flowers, and the massive use of insecticides, the butterfly has become a rarity.

There are more than fifty different species of butterfly breeding in the British Isles. How many have you seen?

We can help this beautiful creature to find a place to feed and breed. A garden, patio or even a large window box can make a substantial difference, if planted with butterflies in mind. Sunny spots with plenty of nectar-laden flowers are what is needed.

There are many plants which you can grow to attract a variety of butterflies, such as candytuft, marigolds, helichrysum, cornflowers and Michaelmas daisies. Flowers with single blooms are the best as they produce the most nectar. Try and visit gardens open to the public and make a note of which plants attract the most butterflies.

If you want the minimum amount of work, then planting perennials is the best idea. These plants keep flowering every year with little or no attention. You may need to thin out the growth occasionally, passing on clumps to your butterfly-loving friends. Aubretia, that lovely purple and pink flowering plant you often see cascading over old stone walls, is an ideal butterfly attracter. The wonderful scented lavender and the useful herb marjoram are also good. Look out for the ice plant, which is a great favourite. Ask for help at your local garden centre.

The best-known plant for butterflies is the buddleia bush, in fact it is often known as the butterfly bush. It is a fast grower, but it can be pruned in the winter. Nettles are perhaps not something you would plant in a window box; however, they will be greatly appreciated if left in the garden.

July

22

The Chinese believe that an aquarium containing six fish brings good fortune and harmony. Western studies have shown that doctors' and dentists' waiting rooms which have aquariums reduce patients' stress.

23

In the primate family, of which there are 179 members, the African gorilla is the largest and the dwarf bush baby is the smallest.

24

The chelonian family has over two thousand species. Tortoises, terrapins and turtles have remained virtually unchanged. But they are all under threat due to human activities.

25

A badger depends a great deal on its superb sense of smell. It is over seven hundred times more powerful than ours. Damp weather is the best for tracking by scent.

26

Herbs for drying should be cut on a dry warm day when they have just started to flower. Dry them in small bunches in circulating air. (Not in the sun or an oven.)

27

Don't forget to feed potted plants regularly in the growing season.

28

The quality of honey is dependent on the food the bees eat. Taste and smell the difference between heather honey and honey produced by bees living near fields of the luminous yellow-flowered oilseed rape.

29

In a hot summer your garden pond will suffer from lack of oxygen. Make sure you keep it free of debris and you could consider circulating the water with a pond pump.

30

Spot the difference. A millipede has a flattened body and is a plant eater and therefore a slow mover. A centipede has a rounded body, is a carnivore and so has to be a fast mover to catch its prey.

31

Every year six million hectares of dry land that could be cultivated becomes desert. The world's deserts used to be covered in plants, and therefore animals too.

SOAR WITH
THE WIND

What is one of the most environmentally friendly, cheap and fun pastimes for people of all ages? FLYING KITES. They are easy to make and can be any size, to suit the 'pilot'. Use your imagination and create a wind-born masterpiece.

You could organize a kite-flying day. Ask the local authority if you can do it in the park, or use the school grounds. Ask local businesses to donate prizes, and charge entry fees. The profits could be donated to a charity promoting alternative energy use e.g. The Centre for Alternative Technology (CAT).

The categories could be as varied as you wish, depending on how many prizes you have: the largest, smallest, most elaborate, highest flyer, most unusual shape, the one created out of the most environmentally friendly materials, oldest and youngest 'pilot' are just a few.

Kite flying can be done by people of all ages and abilities. Why not invite a local group for disabled young people to become involved?

August

1

Around five thousand Icelandic black-tailed godwits spend their winters in the British Isles.

2

Each year around 63 centimetres of rain falls on London. It is a mere drop in a bucket compared to the rainforests. The average fall there is about 400 centimetres, but in the really wet ones 1000 centimetres is likely!

3

A snake's flicking tongue plays a vital part in tracking down prey. In the roof of its mouth, the snake has two sacs which open near the front, called the organs of Jacobson. These organs act like our sense of smell, when they receive messages from the tongue.

4

Try and eat at least three different types of organically grown fresh raw vegetables today. You will be surprised how good they taste. It is healthy for you, and by buying them you are encouraging more to be grown.

5

Wood ants are very sensitive to the weather. They have been seen altering the angle of their nest roof in changing conditions to keep the nest dry.

6

A female cane toad (*Bufo marinus*) can lay up to twenty thousand eggs. This South American toad is much larger than our common toad (*Bufo bufo*), it can reach 24 centimetres in length. It was introduced into Queensland, Australia, in 1935 to combat the beetles which were devastating the sugar-cane crops.

7

The nine-banded armadillo has babies of the same sex throughout its life. It always has four to a litter and they are all identical.

WILDLIFE CASUALTIES

You may find animals and birds suffering from accidental injury or sometimes intentional harm. It is important to take the right steps if it is at all possible to save its life.

The casualty will certainly be in a state of shock. If it is not unconscious then you must handle it as little as possible. Even if the creature is unconscious, you could be making the injuries worse by incorrect handling.

You must also bear in mind that a frightened animal, and even some birds, can be extremely dangerous. Make sure that your face and hands are well protected.

Birds in particular must be kept warm and in a dark box until the correct treatment can be given. Many injured birds die from stress caused by overhandling from a well-meaning person.

Also remember that all wild creatures have their own parasites. Fleas and lice are common, and tend to leave a dying animal as its body temperature decreases. They are not harmful to humans but you may run into trouble if you take them home!

Unlike a doctor for the human animal, a vet has to be familiar with numerous different animals. He may not have had an opportunity to work on the particular wild creature you have found. The Wildlife Hospitals Trust has their own vet and staff with many years' experience of dealing with Britain's wildlife.

Whatever your problem, they have a twenty-four-hour phone number, with someone on duty who can advise you. If you don't live anywhere near them, they will tell you your nearest wild animal hospital, the first aid you can give and possibly the nearest vet with wild-animal experience.

They run a membership scheme for people who would like to help with their work. You can adopt one of the permanent residents, who is not able to be released. They need your used postage stamps and any support and funds you can raise. They also produce fact sheets. Send SAE if you write.

Wildlife Hospitals Trust
1 Pemberton Close
Aylesbury
Buckinghamshire
HP21 7NY

The phone number is 0296 29860

8

The Australian sea snake is the most venomous snake in the world. It is not known to have bitten any people.

9

An easy way to make instant savings on your home's water consumption is to put a brick in your lavatory cistern. If you are having a new one, check that it is the most economic water user available.

10

Find a corner in your garden for some thistles. They are a great source of winter food, especially for goldfinches, who love their seeds. The collective name for a group of goldfinches is a charm.

11

A bluebell wood is most likely a very old wood. The beautiful flowers appear and die before the trees have their thickest summer foliage. A small isolated clump in a hedgerow could indicate where an ancient woodland once stood.

12

Choose food with no additives whenever possible. In Britain we each eat about three kilos of food additives every year. No one really knows the long-term effects of these products.

13

Professor Vo Quy has been awarded the World Wide Fund for Nature's (WWF) International Gold Medal for his work in Vietnam. The war destroyed wildlife and he has set up a scheme to plant 500 million trees a year.

14

If you or your parents have an old pair of binoculars or a telescope you don't use anymore, contact the World Wide Fund for Nature (WWF) on 04868 25545. They desperately need them for field workers in the world's tropical rainforests and wardens in mountainous areas.

NATURAL DEFENCES

For an awful long time most gardeners have been relying on poisonous chemicals to get rid of unwanted pests. More and more efficient pesticides have been developed and have been soaking into the land. Slowly people have realized that this isn't such a good idea and some of the long term ill effects are starting to be noticed. Nature has always had her own defences against harmful creatures and a balance was maintained until the interference by people.

In the wild, plants are never found in strict rows or growing in isolation from each other. Plants develop along side each other and give the predator choices and sometimes confused signals.

Being a green gardener means looking for ways to mimic nature and use natural means to stop plants being destroyed. It means using organic methods, everything you put on the garden should be beneficial.

If you have a garden, get involved in pest control and teach your parents these natural methods:

Greenfly, also known as aphids, are the enemies of rose growers everywhere. Unlike many insects they do not lay eggs but have thousands of babies which commence feeding immediately. The ladybird is one enemy of the aphid and it is possible to buy a box of ladybirds to release into a greenfly infested greenhouse. However it would be silly to do that outdoors as they would fly away. One tip to try is to plant the delicious tasting but evil-smelling garlic in amongst the roses. Apparently aphids hate garlic as much as vampires do! Do not allow the garlic to flower or the smell will ruin your rose perfume.

Slugs eat loads of plants but they also love beer. If you sink a container of beer into the soil in between every few plants they will be found drunk and drowned every morning.

Root fly can ruin a carrot crop but they don't like chives. If you plant alternate carrots and chives it will help keep them away.

See how many more natural ways you can discover to protect your garden.

15

Don't let your parents throw away old clothes, bedding, curtains etc. Take them to your local charity shop. They have arrangements to sell them to recycling plants if they are too old to use again.

16

To care for the world you must care for its inhabitants. To care for others you must also care for yourself. Have a 'be good to yourself day' today. Tell yourself how great you are!

17

The world's largest flower is one metre across. *Rafflesia arnoldii* smells of rotting flesh, and it has no leaves or stalk. It is found in Sabah in northern Borneo and grows on rope-like vines in the rainforests.

18

Kittiwakes have deserted their traditional cliffs to nest on ledges of an old flour mill on the River Tyne at Gateshead. Many birds are adapting to new environments. Look out for them.

19

Twenty per cent of all the wild flowers in the British Isles are threatened with extinction. Around twenty have already disappeared this century. Never pick flowers on a country walk. Leave them to see, and for everyone's pleasure.

20

Hair clippings from you and your dog, bits of wool, teased out string will all be readily recycled by birds as nesting material. Just leave it outside and they will help themselves.

21

There were 54,000 road accidents in the UK in 1989 involving stray animals. It is your responsibility to keep your pets under control, for their own safety as well as everyone else's.

HOLIDAY HELP

In the long school holidays you could take the chance to offer yourself as a plant and pet minder to people your family know. Holiday-makers with dogs and cats are reasonably well catered for. Those with smaller pets sometimes have difficulties.

Caged pets such as budgies, rabbits, hamsters and the like need attention daily. It is essential that they are kept clean and are given fresh food and water.

If you have the space at home and it is all right with your family, then it is easier to bring the animal, cage and all, home — or have the owner deliver it to you. Make sure the owner provides all the food, sawdust, bedding, etc. that the animal will use.

If you have lots of animals to look after, then you will probably take care of them in their own homes. Plants should always be left where they are; they don't like being disturbed.

It is important to make particular notes on the requirements of everything in your care. The responsibility should not be taken lightly.

Decide on your rates for the job beforehand and ask owners to sign a form to give you permission to take the animal to the vet, at their expense, should the need arise. Make a note of the animal's usual vet. The form must also state that you accept no responsibility for accidents and loss.

A portion of your fee could be donated to charity.

CAR WASH

Start a car-wash service in your area. Write out some handbills and deliver them to car owners you know or hand them out in car parks with your parents. Never stick them under car wipers as they usually end up as litter.

State that you will be using only environmentally friendly cleaning products and the minimum of water, unlike the automatic car washes. A percentage of the profit will be donated to charity. (Fill in your chosen charity.) And say that discounts will be given for the following:

Cars using a lead-free petrol.

Cars with a catalytic converter.

Cars with engines of 1600cc or less.

Cars used in a pool system for journey sharing.

Car owners who use bicycles or walk on short journeys.

Of course you should never go into strangers' houses without an adult – even to get fresh water. Make sure you ask your parents if it is all right for you to do this.

August

22

Since the turn of the century, half the ponds in Britain
have disappeared. Around three-quarters of our
remaining ponds are polluted. Ponds situated in shady
areas are least likely to contain a variety of plants and
animals.

23

On hot days, put a few mint sprigs in water next to
open windows. This discourages flies. The old-
fashioned sticky fly strips are the best way to deal
with flies in the home. DON'T SPRAY!

24

In London in 1952 four thousand people died as a
result of air pollution. It was due to this that the
smokeless zones were created.

25

Despite the dramatic changes in the West's relations
with Eastern European countries, the arrival of the
nineties still sees the United States testing nuclear
weapons. An underground test five hundred metres
below the Nevada desert took place in March 1990.

26

The hatching of a Californian condor chick in San Diego Zoo in March 1990 brings the total world population to thirty-three. All of the birds are in captivity, split between the zoos in San Diego and Los Angeles.

27

When walking in the country or in nature reserves, always keep to the footpaths. Use your eyes, ears and noses and not your mouths, and you will see so many more animals and birds.

28

Try smiling at everyone today. Some people will wonder what you have been up to, most people will smile back, and everyone will feel better. Happy is healthy.

29

The echidnas (short and long-beaked) and the platypus are the only members of a strange group of animals. They are monotremes — egg-laying mammals.

30

If you have your daily milk delivered, bring it indoors as soon as possible, or leave a bottle cover for the milkman to use. Sunlight will affect the vitamin B2, destroying as much as ten per cent every hour.

31

Your daily vitamin A and C requirements will be met if you eat one large raw carrot and one orange. Try and eat more raw vegetables. They are nutritious and good for your teeth.

ANIMAL ALPHABET FRIEZE

If you have a younger relative or are soon to have a baby brother or sister then making an animal alphabet frieze is a great present.

You will need a very long strip of strong paper. You can either make this by sticking lots of pieces together with sticky tape or find someone who is going to be doing some wall papering. Very often the wallpaper is too wide for a corner of the room and one long strip is cut from the roll. This is ideal.

Next you need to collect twenty-six pictures of animals representing each letter of the alphabet. You can cut these out of magazines or photograph them. You might have to cheat a bit on some letters — X can be difficult but there is a type of clawed frog called a Xenopus so maybe you could use any frog picture. If you can't think of any animal beginning with a letter of the alphabet, try looking in an encyclopedia. You'll probably find lots more than you ever thought existed.

The space given to each animal on the strip will depend on the size of the picture you have. You can cut out letters to stick on or you can paint or draw them. Once finished it will make a very interesting and attractive present, to decorate a young child's room.

September

1

When you're around farmland, check the cattle-grids
for escape routes for small mammals. Many
hedgehogs become trapped in the bottom of the grid
and often drown in watertight ones. Get permission to
build a stone 'staircase' in one corner.

2

A fully grown tree is used to make every 500
disposable nappies — that's just three months supply
of nappies for one baby.

3

Make sure the wood preservatives used in your
garden and home are the water-based animal-safe
variety.

4

Open drains are deathtraps for wandering wildlife.
Check all drain covers regularly.

5

Cats should not be treated for fleas and worms at the same time. Leave a couple of weeks' gap to avoid the risk of a toxic combination. Always ask the vet if there is a problem.

6

There are only thirty-five native tree species in Great Britain. All the other trees have been brought from other countries.

7

Never keep fish in a goldfish bowl. The water surface is too small to absorb enough oxygen.

HEAPS OF COMPOST

Do you get into trouble with your parents for not eating all your food? You may not always want to finish everything that is on your plate but it needn't be wasted. You can make it into valuable food for the garden, in other words compost. Make it your responsibility to collect all the families' leftovers and kitchen waste. It will take a long time for your compost to be ready for feeding the garden but it means your house will never waste anything again, and your garden will have rich, chemical-free fertiliser.

You can buy ready-made compost bins, but it is much cheaper to make your own. The basic compost bin is an open, airy frame held in place with sturdy wooden sides. To get the best compost, it's essential that air circulates freely all around the compost. Plastic-coated wire is a good basic construction material. Leave one side hinged to make life easy when you need to get at the contents. Don't forget to leave a gap at the base for air movement. This is a bit complicated and you will probably need help to make it properly.

Now for what to put in your compost. All the garden debris, apart from thick woody twigs, should be used. If your family has a bonfire, they can burn the twigs and you can use the ash for your compost heap. Most of the contents of your kitchen bin can end up on the compost heap. Don't use bones as they take too long to decompose. Vegetable peelings, tea, coffee, leftovers (which aren't suitable as bird food), cardboard, wool, hair are all suitable. Use your imagination – so many things will enrich your compost. Good farmyard manure will get the bacteria working and pet droppings will help.

Don't let your compost dry out. Keep it damp, or the bacteria will stop working. Remember to cover the top in heavy rain as too much water is just as harmful. In winter the bins should be insulated against the cold. You can use old carpets or straw bales. Every so often turn it around with a fork.

When your compost is a rich mulchy consistency, it is ready to use. Spread it over the surface of the garden areas your family agree need to be enriched, and let the worms do the work of digging it in.

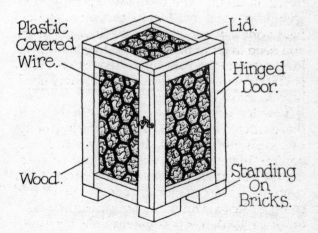

September

8

The domesticated llama is a descendant of the wild guanaco. A South American pack animal, it is related to the camel and shares the unpleasant habit of spitting to show displeasure.

9

A Swedish naturalist, Carolus Linnaeus, devised the original plan to classify every living thing with its own individual Latin name. This work, started in the eighteenth century, allows the scientific community, speaking many different languages, to discuss animals and plants without confusing the common and often different local names.

10

Don't suffer from 'green guilt'. You can't expect to change the world overnight. An ancient proverb says 'A little nonsense, now and then, is relished by the wisest men.'

11

It is never too early to start training a puppy. Watch the 'Dog Care' video (Virgin VBV008).

12

The New World is both the American continents, from the extreme north of Canada to Tierra del Fuego in the south, and all the islands off the mainland, like the Falklands.

13

You can kill a tree if you strip off the bark in a full circle (ring barking) because it is the outer rings which conduct the water up the tree.

14

London Zoo was first open to members in 1828. By 1847 it was open to anyone who could afford the one-shilling entrance fee (sixpence on Monday).

SOCK-PUPPETS

Recycle all the odd socks which are left after the laundry has been done. Put on your own environmental puppet shows telling stories of animals' welfare. Fill out the nose ends with cut up tights or scraps.

Draw nostrils and eyes in place with black felt tip.

Horse.

Pieces Of Felt For Ears.

Black sock. White wool or button to make eyes. Whiskers: black wool.

Sea Lion.

See how many more you can think of. Towelling socks make great lambs. You can also invent creatures. How about making a tartan sock into a haggis animal?

Buttons for eyes, cloth for ears, black wool for nose. Do loads of over stitching to make it bigger.

Dog.

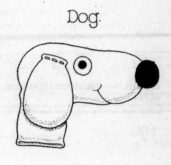

Cut the sock open along this line. Flatten out the top and bottom halves and stick them to the card to make the duck's beak. Paint the inside of the card yellow. Leave holes in between the card and sock to insert your thumb and forefinger so you can operate the beak.

Duck.

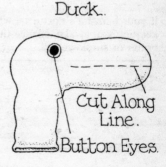

Cut Along Line.

Button Eyes.

September

15

Cage birds should have natural perches. Replace the smooth dowel perches with fruit tree branches — good for feet and beak exercises. Renew them as required. All seed eaters need good-quality mineral grit.

16

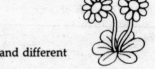

Britain has eighteen thousand different plant species.

17

If your hamster's nocturnal wheel-exercising is keeping you awake, silence the wheel with a little butter or sunflower oil.

18

The outside leaves of a lettuce contain up to fifty times more carotene than the paler heart. We convert carotene into vitamin A.

19

The largest moth in Britain is the emperor moth. The females are up to nine centimetres across, and as they are mainly nocturnal, they can be mistaken for bats.

20

Think before you order an 'exotic' meal. Bird's nest, shark's fin and turtle soups and frogs' legs are not fancy names for something else.

21

If your house plant leaves are turning yellow but not dropping you may be watering with hard water. Use rainwater or boil the tap water.

AUTUMN LEAVES

Collecting leaves during the autumn is a lovely way to spend some free time. Try to find all sorts of different shapes that have come down whole from the trees. If you just keep them around the house they soon dry out and eventually crumble, so here is something else to do with them.

Leaf pictures are easy to make and lovely to look at. If you collect leaves now, you could take this opportunity to plan early for Christmas and start making some very individual and beautiful presents.

See if you can find some old picture frames with glass in them. Perhaps there are some old ones your parents have stored away or you might get some cheaply at a jumble sale. Perhaps you have an old picture you have grown out of which you could use the frame of. Peel off the sticking tape at the back and take out the picture inside. Clean the frame and paint it if you want. Get the glass spotlessly clean with lots of hot soapy water but take great care when you are washing it or ask your parents to clean it for you — wet glass is slippery and dangerous.

Cut out a piece of black card to fit inside the frame (you can cover ordinary cardboard with a piece of black paper), and arrange your leaves in an attractive pattern on the black card. Keep to colours that go well with each other. Lay the sheet of glass over the top to hold them in place, then fit the glass and cardboard, with the leaves sandwiched in between, into the frame, and tape it down at the back with sticky tape. Do not glue the leaves in position or this will show up on the glass. It's a good idea to practise a few times with old leaves before you finally tape your picture down.

September

22

On the planet Earth, one hundred and fifty babies are born every minute

23

The tropical rainforests have eighty per cent of the world's known insects.

24

More than thirty thousand people die every year from rabies.

25

There is almost no soil in a tropical rainforest. The plants grow on a layer of decomposed fallen wood and leaves. Once the trees are felled, the rainforest rapidly loses this layer and becomes a barren wasteland.

26

The outer Hebrides are the breeding sites for one hundred and four different species of bird.

27

Cranes have returned to nest in Britain. The RSPB anounced that the birds have been trying to breed at a secret location since 1981. They have managed to raise young three times. These birds stopped breeding in Britain around 1600 when hunters finally wiped them out.

28

We CAN make a difference to what happens in our world. Each of us can set an example. A successful pressure group is only made up of a lot of caring individuals.

29

In a good 'food year' the harvest mouse can be a very prolific breeder. Their nests are made from dead stems woven into tall grasses, and may be home to four broods – with up to nine young in each.

30

We must not forget that the rainforests are also home to many different tribes of people. They all depend on the forests and only take what they need to survive. Their unique life styles must be protected.

GREEN GRAFFITI

Random painting and scribbling on walls and doors is unsightly and can be dangerous. It is also very expensive to remove. Having the freedom to paint and draw over a large area is fun and can look very attractive.

Ask permission from your school or local church hall or perhaps even the library to have a Green Graffiti wall.

All you need is an old roll of wallpaper. There may be one at your home or you can buy a very cheap odd roll from the 'end of line' bin at the decorating shop.

Put the wallpaper up and invite people to cover it with drawings, paintings, poems, sayings — anything they like.

Fix the wallpaper securely but make sure you don't use something that will damage the surface of the wall. Put the paper at a reasonable height for most people to work on.

Choose a title for the overall picture, with a green theme. It could be 'Rainforest' or 'Whales' or even 'Rubbish'. There are loads of others to use. Write the title above it to help inspire people.

Make people aware that the wall is there and you are inviting them to participate. It is best if you can organize set times for your painting sessions, as you can be sure things are clean and tidy afterwards.

Tell your local newspaper what you are doing and how you feel about your local world. You may influence others to start thinking too.

October

1

According to Friends of the Earth, over a quarter of a tonne of plutonium – a dangerous chemical – has been deposited in the Irish Sea from Sellafield nuclear plant.

2

Dinosaurs were on the earth for 140 million years. Their name (*Dinosauria*) was given to them by Richard Owen, the first superintendent of the Natural History Museum.

3

The Maori people of New Zealand have many tribal legends about the creation of the earth. The Earth Mother is known as Papa, and the sky is known as Rangi. They combined to create life.

4

Two handfuls of peanuts contain your daily requirement of vitamin B3.

5

If you live near an animal sanctuary, they may be interested in taking your old newspapers. Quite often these organizations are also keen to have blankets and towels.

6

Try and spend some time with people who make you happy. Mark Twain said 'Grief can take care of itself, but to get the full value of joy, you must have somebody to divide it with.'

7

Look out for products containing jojoba oil. This Mexican shrub produces the perfect substitute for sperm-whale oil.

NESTING IN SAFETY

Since the massive tree losses from hurricanes and with the disappearance of more and more old buildings, it is more vital than ever to provide nesting boxes and sites for birds. Put them up in October and they will serve as winter roosts and be well established by the next breeding season.

The Royal Society for the Protection of Birds has quite a selection of different nest boxes and artificial nests, such as those for house martins, for sale by mail order. Send a large SAE to RSPB The Lodge, Sandy, Beds SG19 2DL, for a sales list.

With adult help, making a fairly basic nest box isn't too difficult, and if you can get the wood from a demolition site it will be very cheap. Well matured thick wood is best, old floor boards or similar, treated with creosote. The RSPB issue a leaflet on how to construct a nesting box and they will send it to you, free of charge, if you write to the address given above and ask for one. Do enclose a self addressed envelope.

Putting the boxes in good areas is important. They must be safe from predators. Avoid too much direct sunlight or too much shade, and don't have the open side facing the prevailing wind. Tilt the roof forward to allow rain to drip away from the opening. Don't fasten the boxes permanently to their sites as you may want to move them, and you will need to clean them out each year. Vary hole sizes and have some open fronts to attract different birds. Always fasten a piece of wood to a building first and then attach the box to the wood. The box will then remain dry with the air circulation between it and the wall. Use wire to fasten boxes to trees; don't hammer into the trunk.

Old kettles, bits of drainpipe, plant pots, empty half-coconuts – all sorts of weird receptacles have been used by birds, so hang some around your garden. Chicken wire around bushes and over creepers that are likely nest sites will keep predators out and allow the birds in. At the end of the breeding season, remove all the old nesting material, clean the box and dust with pyrethrum powder to control parasites.

October

8

The London Tunnel Ring Main will move over a
thousand million litres of water per day, when it is
finally completed.

9

Unlike humans, crocodiles have teeth which continue
to grow throughout their life, with the new teeth
pushing out the old.

10

Looking for an unusual present? Why don't you adopt
a duck at your nearest wildfowl trust.

11

You are an extremely important and powerful person.
Make sure you channel your energy in the right
direction. Be good to yourself and others. Take care of
your health and use your strength to achieve the best
results in whatever you decide to do.

12

Noise can cause severe stress. Please don't be a noise polluter. Think of others before you play loud music. Insulation in your home not only saves energy but stops sound carrying.

13

Think twice before you pay to see a circus or a dolphin show. Performing animals are not entertaining, if you really consider that they are being held in captivity for your entertainment.

14

If you want to give some of the seeds from your wild-flower garden to a friend, remember to collect them when they are fresh. Dry them slowly in a low temperature, along with some silica gel. Once they're dry, store them in heavy polythene bags. They'll keep in the fridge for years until you find suitable sites.

SET UP A BIRD TABLE

A bird table can be a very simple affair, or as grand as the Ritz. You could make your own with the help of a parent by simply nailing a square piece of wood to the top of a pole (which you then fix firmly into the ground) or you could persuade your parents to buy one at a garden centre or pet shop. Or why not ask for one for your birthday?

If you are making your own bird table, and the person who is helping you is skilful with tools, it is a good idea to have a roof on your table to protect the food in severe weather. The position of the table is very important; you need to have a good view from your house to get the maximum pleasure from your visitors, and they need to be safe. Don't put the table too close to any likely hiding places for predators. Leave space around the base for easy cleaning and for scattering food for ground feeders.

It is best to move the table a couple of times a year to avoid the build-up of droppings, which can give birds diseases and worm infestation. It is very important to clean the table frequently and remove stale food.

Don't be discouraged if your new bird table doesn't attract a hungry horde immediately. It often takes a few weeks for the local population to get the message. Offer a wide variety of food and you will greatly increase the number of different species visiting your table. See the next project for tips on what food to give them.

Squirrels can be real pests, stealing every scrap of food as soon as you put it out. Leave some food for them at the other end of the garden. Preventing them from reaching the bird table can be a problem. One way is to fasten a bulky circle of gorse and hawthorn halfway up the pole. There are purpose-built devices for keeping the squirrels away from the bird food, and these are available from garden centres.

Starlings, pigeons and gulls are great opportunists and will leave nothing for the smaller birds such as the tits. Use various nut and seed holders suspended from the table, and the tiny more agile birds will get their share.

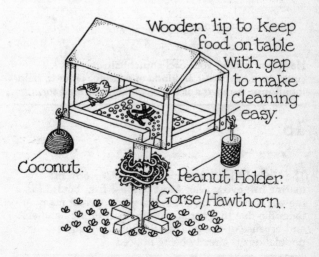

Wooden lip to keep food on table With gap to make cleaning easy.

Coconut.

Peanut Holder.

Gorse/Hawthorn.

15

When using your local bottle bank
remember to remove any bottle tops before
making your deposit. If it has separate
colour bins, have your bottles already
sorted.

16

Whatever colour scheme you have in your bathroom,
insist on using only white recycled loo paper. Some of
the dyes used in the manufacture of coloured varieties
are poisonous to fish.

17

Have you visited you local churchyard recently? It
could be a haven for all kinds of wildlife. Offer to help
monitor or manage it if it looks totally uncared for.

18

The United Kingdom imports £750,000 worth of
marine fish every year. Most of these fish, bound for
the pet trade, are caught in the wild. A great many of
them die due to ignorance on the part of the handlers
and because of stress. The effect on the wild
populations is already being noticed.

19

The acacia bush uses ants to protect itself. The hollow thorns provide them with homes and they feed on the plant's nectar. In return they attack possible enemies such as caterpillars.

20

If there is always water left in the kettle after your family have made a pot of tea, you are wasting energy by boiling too much.

21

The reedbeds of Leighton Moss in Lancashire are home to the bird with an unbelievably loud call. The BOOM of the male bittern can be heard at great distances. It is estimated that there are less than thirty birds left in Britain, making it one of our rarest.

BIRD FOOD AND WATER

Once you have a bird table in your garden make sure you feed the birds regularly, as once your feeding station is established, 'your' birds will come to depend on you — especially in the coldest weather. Food with a high fat content is particularly useful to many of our smallest birds. They need to consume vast quantities of food. If the food you offer is high-energy food, they will benefit much more, as they will be using less of their own stored energy in the action of feeding.

Always buy seeds from a reputable dealer. It is much cheaper if you buy in bulk, so why not get together with a few friends and split the load? Quantities over 25 kilos are usually delivered free. All peanuts should have the Bird Food Standards Mark. This ensures the nuts are not contaminated with Aflatoxin. This was responsible for killing many wild birds.

Half-coconuts and split marrowbones can give hours of feeding if you hang them from the table. You can put out a poultry carcass but make sure you tie it to the table. A fallen carcass would be a great hazard to your pet dog.

Make a 'bird cake' in the empty coconut shell or in a plant or yoghurt pot. Under adult supervision, gently melt suet or other solid fat in a pan. Add assorted seeds, raisins, sultanas, and any other scraps. Pour into your container with the string attached and let it set, then hang it from the table.

Start feeding the birds in September if the weather is bad and feed them through until the end of April or longer if the weather doesn't warm up. NEVER FEED THEM: salted nuts or desiccated coconut. Soak white bread before feeding.

Wholemeal bread, porridge oats, fruit and kitchen scraps such as bacon rind will all be enjoyed by the birds.

Water is essential for all birds. Fresh water should be supplied at least once a day. Bathing is vital for feather maintenance. Healthy feathers keep the bird well insulated through the long cold winter nights. Never add anything to the water to stop it freezing.

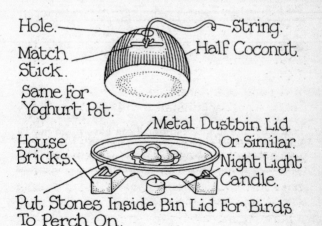

Hole.— —String.
Match Stick. Half Coconut.
Same For Yoghurt Pot.

House Bricks. Metal Dustbin Lid Or Similar. Night Light Candle.

Put Stones Inside Bin Lid For Birds To Perch On.

October

22

Since 1988 ten bearded vultures have been released in the French Alps. Twelve birds have been released in Austria. The captive breeding programme, started in the 1970s in European zoos, was developed to reintroduce the almost extinct bird back to its native habitat.

23

Ninety-six per cent of the lowland gorilla population of the People's Republic of Zaire has been wiped out in the last two hundred years. Humans are the culprits, for destroying forests and hunting the gorillas.

24

Half a hectare of forest in Brazil can have up to five hundred different species of trees in it. An area the size of Britain is damaged or destroyed every year.

25

Diabetes is not only a human illness. Many animals suffer from it, including a giant tortoise from the Galapagos.

26

Hundreds of thousands of birds use Britain's estuaries as a rest stop during migration. Developers are seriously threatening these unique and vital habitats. Eighty are at risk and twenty-eight are in severe danger.

27

An adult healthy dog is quite happy with one well-balanced meal a day. Do not feed it fattening titbits. Puppies, pregnant bitches and bitches with puppies should have more food, with added vitamins and calcium.

28

Rabies is a highly infectious killer. Never attempt to smuggle any living creature into this country. When on holiday abroad, avoid personal contact with animals. Britain is rabies-free — let's make sure we keep it that way.

29

Throughout the country over one thousand nest boxes have been located to attract dormice. Once the dormouse was a favourite food, kept in stone jars and over fed. It would sleep for months on end if kept cool, so it provided fresh meat.

30

To prevent falling leaves from fouling your pond water, make a cover with netting on a frame. Leaves placed on garden borders will inhibit weed growth by keeping out the light.

31

Elephants communicate with each other over long distances using infrasonic calls. Because these sounds are too low for humans to hear, elephants were once thought to have some kind of telepathic communication.

TREES FOR FREE

Every autumn, an old chap I know gathers acorns and other 'seeds' of our native trees and hedges. He keeps half to put out as winter feed for animals and birds and the other half he plants. Over the seventy plus years of his life he must have been responsible for planting thousands of trees and bushes. What a marvellous monument to leave behind.

He collects old plant pots and other suitable containers and has a continuous flow of seeds in and plants out. In his small garden he has plants of all ages. A simple cold frame, made from old floorboards and window frames, protects the very young plants. His compost heap provides the feed, and in return for young trees or bushes, grateful gardeners keep him supplied with potting compost.

Just think if you started now to grow young trees in pots and planted them out when they got bigger, what a difference you could make in your lifetime to the total tree population of Britain.

What's more, every Christmas, birthday or special occasion your gift problem would be solved. You can grow more fancy trees as presents from avocado, lemon and orange pips.

November

1

Each living thing has a unique 'genetic fingerprint'. Most of our DNA (that's the name for the combination of cells that make up our body) is the same, but the order of 'minisatellites' in the nuclei of your body cells is different from everyone else's.

2

After the last Ice Age, some of the first mammals to appear in the British Isles were bats. Contact the Nature Conservancy Council for more information about one of our most misunderstood residents.

3

A Philippine 'petroleum nut' tree can produce fifty litres of oil, suitable for lighting and cooking, every year.

4

Find out how old your local hedgerows are. Count the different kinds of tree and shrub in a 30-metre length. Each different species represents 100 years of hedge growth; i.e. 5 types = a 500-year-old hedgerow. In the last 40 years we have lost 200 kilometres of hedgerow from Britain. That's five times the length of the Equator!

5

Hundreds of millions of birds are killed each year whilst attempting to migrate over the countries bordering the Mediterranean. The birds are then sold as pets or eaten, depending on what they are. Nets, traps and shooting, often just for 'fun' are used by hundreds of thousands of people. Nothing in flight is spared.

6

The temperature at which some species of reptiles' eggs are incubated, determines the sex of the hatchlings. For example, the Nile crocodile's eggs will produce all females if incubated at 31°C and below. However at 34°C and above all males will be the result.

7

Gulls believe in safety in numbers when roosting for the night. They prefer to settle on water well away from the shore, to avoid predators. During the day they will often fly long distances to locate food. Thirty-kilometre trips are not uncommon.

COMPUTER CLOSE-UP

Are you spending loads of time sitting in front of a computer or video game screen?

What kind of lighting have you got to see it by?

How is your posture being affected?

What is your seating like?

Is your terminal at a comfortable working height?

What else are you missing out on?

Are there times when you do not know how long you have been at the screen?

VDUs (visual display units − like a computer screen) generate low-level radiation. Prolonged exposure to any kind of radiation is not good for us. People complain of eye-strain, headaches, backache and general tiredness when they work with computers.

It is easy to become so involved in a computer game that you lose track of time. If you find you do this, limit yourself to a set period, set an alarm clock and stick to it.

You should have a completely adjustable seat. This must support your spine, and your feet should be able to rest comfortably on the floor.

The working surface should be adjusted so your arms are as relaxed as possible and your shoulders are not hunched up.

The VDU should be in a position where there is a lot of natural light, but it must not reflect off the screen. If you need artificial light, try and have full-spectrum lighting. This duplicates sunlight and is the most beneficial.

Fix a protective screen to your VDU (phone Environmental Office Systems for details).

Don't leave the terminal switched on when you are not using it.

Use recycled paper for printing.

DO SOMETHING ELSE!

November

8

Bird boxes are homes to much more than their intended occupants. Earwigs, woodlice, spiders and even mice are all likely to be found inside. Clean out your boxes each year at the end of the breeding season but before the winter. Many birds like to use them as cosy winter roosting places.

9

Fish have been around for 500 million years. Modern humans have been here for about 35,000 years. Fish live in the Antarctic in water at sub-zero temperatures and in thermal springs at over 40°C. About 20,000 different species are known to science.

10

Parts of the Amazonian rainforest in Brazil have remained undisturbed for over one hundred million years. The temperate forests of Europe and North America have only been around since the last Ice Age, eleven million years ago.

11

Try and do something nice today without being asked. The German poet Goethe said, 'Kindness is the golden chain by which society is bound together.'

12

Candlelight is soothing. Persuade your family to have supper by candlelight. The candle's light is increased by standing it in front of a mirror.

13

Try hanging millet sprays out for your wild birds. Binding them lengthwise to a clothesline stops them breaking off.

14

Save water by having showers and keep a bath for a treat. Don't leave taps running. In dry weather, use old bathwater to water the garden. A detachable hose can be connected to the outflow pipe of the drain.

WHICH WAY DOES THE WIND BLOW?

Walk around your house with a lit candle to find the draughts. Are your fuel bills very high? Is your household wasting loads of energy? Could you help an elderly neighbour cut their heating bill? Spend today checking around the house for heat-loss areas. Draught-proofing around doors and windows is easy to apply. Make a draught snake to lie along the bottom of doors and cut out icy floor draughts. Cover your letterbox with a rectangle of stiff plastic (you can cut a piece out of a flooring tile if you have any left over after tiling your floor).

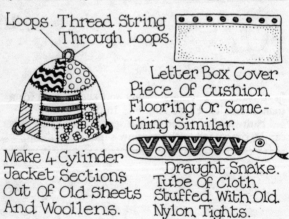

Loops. Thread String Through Loops.

Letter Box Cover. Piece Of Cushion Flooring Or Something Similar.

Make 4 Cylinder Jacket Sections Out Of Old Sheets And Woollens.

Draught Snake. Tube Of Cloth Stuffed With Old Nylon Tights.

Make an extra cylinder jacket for the hot water tank — thick padding can save an amazing amount of energy. Cut out eight shapes roughly fitting a quarter side of your tank each. Use old sheets to make them, or, if you haven't got old sheets, sew together any old scraps of material. They don't have to look good, just do the job! Sew the shapes together in pairs so that you have four cases and fill them up with old woollen clothes. Sew loops on the corners, then tie them together round the tank. Doing it like this means you don't have to make a perfect fitted jacket and there are slits available for the pipes and taps to poke through. Cut other bits of old, warm clothing into strips and use them to wrap round your hot water pipes. This also helps keep the heat in.

15

Wolf packs roamed England until the time of Henry VII, and only disappeared from Scotland in the eighteenth century.

16

Coral grows only a few centimetres a year. Please don't buy any as a holiday souvenir. Avoid buying all shells and dried sea creatures.

17

Kiwis incubate their eggs longer than any other bird. The female lays two eggs weighing approximately a third of her body weight and the male sits on them for around ninety days.

18

The jay's habit of burying acorns in times of plenty has been one of the ways in which the oak tree spread. The French name, *geai des chenes*, means oakjay.

19

Keeping fish as a hobby was mentioned by
Samuel Pepys in his famous diaries.

20

Twenty different wildflowers have become extinct in
Britain this century.

21

If you see oil on or near the beach, telephone the
nearest coastguard immediately.

HEDGEHOG HOMES

A hedgehog is a great asset to any garden. It consumes vast quantities of garden 'pests' and is completely harmless. It has quite a reputation as a flea bearer, but its fleas do not go on people.

If you are lucky enough to have a hedgehog regularly visiting your garden and you would like it to stay, then why not leave food out and build a hedgehog den? If you have not got your 'own' hedgehog, then you could try and encourage one with the right food.

The best food to leave each night is canned dog or cat food. Bread and cow's milk are not at all suitable. Hedgehogs are carnivores, so bread is not appropriate; they are unable to digest cow's milk properly, and it can be lethal to them.

A hedgehog must have easy access to and from your garden, so there should be regular gaps around the base of your fence or wall. The den should be a waterproof structure about the size of half a tea chest. Decide with your family where it should go. Stand it on bricks half set into the earth, to allow air circulation. Make a ten-centimetre hole in one side of the wooden cube about ten centimetres from the base, and fix a sixty-centimetre-length of drainpipe to it. The pipe must slope downwards to stop water pouring into the box when it rains.

Cover the whole structure with a sheet of polythene and put some dry leaves or straw in the box. Now is the time to make it blend into your garden. Pile soil up over the den and then build a rockery, remembering to leave gaps in the rock for toads and other small creatures.

Ask the gardeners in your family not to use slug pellets. The poisoned slugs will kill a hedgehog.

For more hedgehog information, send a large SAE to

The Wildlife Hospital Trust
1 Pemberton Close
Aylesbury
Buckinghamshire
HP21 7NY

Phone 0296 29860 for help with injured or sick hedgehogs.

November

22

You may read or hear a frequently used green phrase, 'the precautionary principle'. It means: give the environment the benefit of the doubt. If there is the slightest risk damage will occur, don't do it.

23

More than five and half thousand postmen and women are attacked by dogs every year. Take your dog to training classes if he is difficult to control.

24

A ten-centimetre diameter mushroom is capable of producing 1,600,000,000 spores during its short life.

25

The western Scottish island of Islay (pronounced eyelay) is the winter home to twenty thousand barnacle geese. Greenland white-fronted geese also make the long journey to overwinter on this beautiful island.

26

Always leave some dead wood in your garden. The resulting insect inhabitants will encourage many more birds and mammals to visit your home.

27

Are there mice in your house? Use a humane 'live trap' to catch them. The traps are available from good pet shops. The caught mice can be released unharmed, well away from your home.

28

The United States Cancer Institute has identified 3,000 rainforest plants, and discovered that 70 per cent of them have anti-cancer properties.

November

29

Worldwide, one billion people depend on water from the tropical forests for their crops. Ethiopia has lost seven-eighths of its forest coverage in the last forty years.

30

The sperm whale is a master diver. In search of its diet of squid and fish, it has been known to reach depths of 3,193 metres. They are also long-lived (if allowed to), reaching ages of eighty years and even older.

LET THE LIGHT IN

The more natural light entering the house, the less electricity is needed to illuminate it. Large south-facing windows also contribute to the heating, using solar energy. It is therefore important to keep the windows clean.

Offer to help cleaning windows at home. Perhaps you could help an elderly neighbour to keep theirs clean. It may be possible to start your own window-cleaning round, donating some of the proceeds to charity.

What you use to clean the windows is important. For dirty exterior windows, try Ecover washing-up liquid and one of those rubber things, like a windscreen wiper, you see professional window cleaners use. For the inside of windows, use white vinegar and water in equal parts. Spray on with one of those sprays you use to mist plants, and wipe off with clean rags or newspaper. You can add some lemon juice to improve the smell. Don't ever use ladders without adult supervision.

Remember to clean light bulbs and light shades regularly. It is surprising how much dirt they collect, and this cuts down on their efficiency.

December

1

To collect worms for your compost heap, leave a slate or similar flat object on a path near the soil. Look under it regularly, especially after it has been raining.

2

Madagascar is home to many unique animals. One, the hairy-eared dwarf lemur, was thought to be extinct but has been found alive. However its habitat is being destroyed. The hairy-eared dwarf lemur is the world's second smallest primate.

3

Find out where your nearest bottle bank is and use it. If it is too far away, write to your local council and ask for one nearer home. In the meantime get your friends to save bottles too, and make the longer journey worthwhile.

4

Plutonium 239, one of the most toxic substances known to man, has a radioactive half-life of 24,000 years. It is just one of the lethal waste products dumped into the sea from coastal nuclear power plants.

5

Strip heather burning on the moors is vital for a variety of bird and mammal inhabitants. Grouse only feed on young heather, and the different density and growth in each strip provides food and shelter for other moorland creatures.

6

Like human fingerprints, the Bewick swan's black and yellow beak patterns are unique to each bird. This fact makes keeping a record of their habits a lot easier than with most birds. One of the best known was Lancelot, who spent every winter for twenty-three years at the Slimbridge Wildfowl Trust.

7

Block up the fireplace flue when it is not in use. Loads of heat is lost, rising straight up the chimney.

TOKONOMA

The Japanese have some of the worst environment records in the world, which seems a little strange as they also revere nature. Buddhism arrived in Japan in the sixth century and the Buddhist custom of making an offering of flowers and sometimes written scrolls in one special alcove of the house has developed over the years, and now the alcove or *tokonoma* has become a place to display beautiful objects, flower arrangements and bonsai trees.

You don't have to be Japanese or a Buddhist to have your own *tokonoma*. It is easy in the western world to get caught up in the fast pace of life; even in the Green movement. Of course many issues are urgent, but we must also take some time to stop and appreciate what we have.

There must be a corner in your home which could be your *tokonoma*. It does not have to be an alcove, it could be a small windowsill or even a shelf. Keep the space clean and simple, and restrict the number of items. Each week change the display, to remind you and those who see it that the world is full of beautiful things and it is worth preserving.

Here are a few suggestions for inclusion. Use your imagination and your heart and you will find many more.

One beautiful flower, shells collected from the beach, a piece of driftwood, a rock or fossil, autumn leaves, berries, conkers, dried seed heads, feathers, a photograph or painting, a single piece of fruit, a plant. You can try your own version of calligraphy and copy out a wise saying or beautiful verse.

When preparing your *tokonoma*, do so at a quiet time and think about what you are doing. Really look at the structure of each item. Feel the texture of the piece of wood or whatever it is you are working with. Smell the perfume of the flower. Look again each day and feed your soul.

8

Make sure your family never lights a garden bonfire without turning it over first. Many animals see the pile of wood and debris as an ideal home. It is particuarly important in winter, when creatures such as hedgehogs could be hibernating there. And don't light a fire unsupervised.

9

Regularly check the condition of your wild bird food containers. The wire-tube peanut holder should be cleaned out and examined for loose wire, which is liable to trap the bird's legs or pierce their feet.

10

Mangrove forests act as vital nurseries for thousands of different species of marine life.

11

About ninety-five per cent of the ingredients which are used to make cosmetics have been tested on animals at some time. The genuine green cosmetic companies such as Beauty Without Cruelty do not use ingredients which have been tested on animals in the last five years.

12

According to American scientists, the saliva of the vampire bat is aiding the treatment of potential heart attack victims. It is used to break down the blood clots which can cause heart attacks.

13

Do you carry a donor card? Why not discuss the pros and cons with your parents?

14

Oil is recyclable. Seven hundred litres of oil suitable for lubricating or heating can be refined from every thousand litres of treated waste oil. Telephone your local authority for your nearest collection point.

PET SHOW

Why don't you organize a pet show? It would be great if you could do it at school but if not you can do it among your friends. Once you know where it is to take place you can decide whether to include cats and dogs or just to restrict it to pets in cages.

Make a programme with all the details including the number of different classes, and a tear-out entry form. Try and get some prizes donated and make some rosettes. Charge a small entry fee for each class and donate the profit to a local animal charity. Ask someone involved in the charity if they have time to come and be a judge at your show.

Examples of classes:

Smallest animal
Largest animal
Prettiest pet
Hairiest animal
Most beautiful eyes
Most unusual pet
Healthiest looking animal
Owner with the most knowledge about their
  pet's welfare
There are loads more you can think of.

Make rosettes yourself for your pet show winners. Cut out two circles of cardboard for each rosette, by drawing round a small glass or jar and cutting out the shapes. Write '1st' (or '2nd' or '3rd') on one circle and stick a safety pin to the other with sticky tape. Get some ribbon (maybe you have some left over from Christmas or a birthday) and pleat it into a circle of points. Stitch round the ribbon or use double sided tape to hold it in place, then stick the circles either side of the ribbons in the middle so that the points stick out between them. Finally, cut out two short pieces of ribbon and stick them so that they dangle from the bottom of the rosette. To make it look really professional, cut a triangle shape out of the end of each dangling piece of ribbon to give it the proper points.

Safety Pin.   Pleated Ribbon.

Card.

With Extra Ribbon Stuck On Inside.

15

Eat an orange today and plant the pips. Give them plenty of space in damp compost and enclose the pot in a polythene bag, opening it occasionally to let the air circulate. You should see shoots in four weeks or so.

16

Use lemon juice to stop grated apple from turning brown before you add it to your muesli.

17

Choose organic whole grains to avoid chemical contamination.

18

Caged pet birds need access to bathing water. Small birds are happy with a shallow rough-surfaced dish. Parrots and other larger birds need regular spraying. Use a plant spray with tepid water. Give the bird a good soak, and space to preen and dry. Take time to get the bird used to the spray.

 **19**

Kitchen foil stuck on the walls behind each radiator, shiny side facing the wall, saves heat. A great deal of warmth is lost through the walls and the foil reflects it back.

20

Try some herbal tea today. There are loads of different ones and they are better for you than ordinary tea or coffee.

21

Buy a mains adaptor for your radio or cassette player, and use it whenever possible. Batteries produce a fiftieth of the energy it takes to make them.

COMIC CLUB

It is very important to use things over and over again. As we already know, recycling is a valuable conservation aid but re-use is the best one.

Do you normally buy your comics and read them and throw them away or maybe send them to the recycling plant?

How about forming a comic club with your friends? It is a great way to save money and to save the planet's resources.

Decide between you who is going to buy which comic, so that there is no duplication. Set a time limit on how long each of you has to read one comic before you pass it on. The club size will be determined on how many different comics you all want to read. Bear in mind if the club is too large it will be some time before you get the comics and they will be a bit out of date.

Make sticky labels to put on the front of each comic with a list, in order, of the people who are going to read it next. As each person reads the comic they will tick off their names. This way it makes sure no one is missed out.

And when you've all finished with them, you can take them to your local doctor's surgery or dentist's waiting room. That way even more children are getting a chance to use them.

HOST YOUR OWN QUIZ

Television quiz shows are extremely popular and so are quizzes in pubs and even some radio stations have phone-in quiz shows.

You could start your own quiz game by using all the information in this book. Organize your friends and family into teams and get them to compete against each other. Start by using this book to write your questions. Have different question rounds on topics like flowers, animals, birds, trees. Do more reading on the different topics to vary your questions. Try and relate the whole thing to making everyone more aware of their environment.

Establish a point system and play over several weeks to find the overall champion.

Perhaps the losers could be given forfeits. They must complete tasks involving the projects on the GREENDAY pages. For example the person scoring the least should pick up twenty pieces of litter the next day. The second lowest score should pick up fifteen and so on.

December

22

Don't buy nest boxes with perches attached. The bird doesn't need a perch so close and it could be used by a predator to reach the eggs and young.

23

The great bustard stopped breeding in Britain over fifty years ago. Since 1950 only twenty have been seen on our shores.

24

When you are boiling water for cooking purposes on gas or electric rings, bring the water to the boil in the kettle first. It is quicker and cheaper, saving valuable energy.

25

Using newspaper to insulate a floor before laying a carpet saves heat loss and helps to soundproof.

26

Gardeners should not use peat to keep sandy soil moist, but shred newspaper and dig it in.

27

The three-banded white-tailed common bumblebee has the longest tongue of all our native bees. In return for the nectar it takes from flowers, it carries pollen from one to another.

28

Most plastic products on the market today are made from oil. Oil is a nonrenewable resource. Plastics are extremely difficult to recycle. Buy products made from natural materials instead.

December

29

There are around fourteen million gardens in Britain.
If each garden had a wildlife area, just think of the
difference it could make.

30

Bottlebanks were first used in Britain in 1977.

31

Many of our garden plants originate from plants
collected in exotic locations. In the New World there
are five hundred different species of passionflower.

GREEN CHRISTMAS

As your present to the planet think how you can make your Christmas more friendly to the environment.

Here are a few suggestions you may like to try:

Do you really need to eat a turkey? If you do, can you buy a free range one?

Make your presents by recycling other things.

Make your Christmas cards and gift tags by using last year's cards. Cut out pieces and make collage cards and individual shaped tags.

Open presents carefully and re-use the paper and bows.

Invite lonely people to share your Christmas.

Don't forget to feed the birds.

Don't have a real tree.

Be happy but remember the other parts of the world where what you have would be unbelievable.

Try to choose toys without batteries.

Help around the house, Christmas is hard work for parents.

HAVE A VERY HAPPY, PEACEFUL AND LOVING CHRISTMAS.

Find out more

If you don't know what is happening you can't influence the outcome. Read as much as you can about the environment. There are new publications coming out all the time. Try and form a reading pool with your friends and swop books and magazines. Look into creating green groups at school.

Join as many green organizations as you can, and you will get regular bulletins of their work.

It doesn't matter if you are not old enough to vote, you will be one day. Politicians, like bank managers, are very aware of young people, believing if they can capture you early, they will have you for life. Now this may or may not be true, but it does mean they will listen to you. Use this to ask questions, and make sure you get answers. Write to your Member of Parliament if you don't agree with what is happening, and encourage your friends to do the same.

Remember the world begins at your front door. The consequences of actions on your immediate surroundings fan out like ripples in a pool, and add to the total good or bad. It's up to you.

Useful addresses

Thank you to all the following for keeping me up to date with the world's problems:

Remember always to enclose an SAE when writing to a charity.

Friends of the Earth
26–28 Underwood Street
London   N1 7JQ   phone 081 200 0200

Greenpeace
30–31 Islington Green
London   N1 8XE

Alternative Technology Association
Centre for Alternative Technology
Machynlleth
Powys   SY20 9AZ   phone 0654 2400

The Wildlife Hospitals Trust
1 Pemberton Close
Aylesbury
Buckinghamshire
HP21 7NY   phone 0296 29860

The Conservation Foundation
1 Kensington Gore
London   SW7 2AR   phone 071 823 8842

Young Ornithologists Club
Royal Society for the Protection of Birds
The Lodge
Sandy
Bedfordshire   SG19 2DL   phone 0767 680551

**Royal Society for the
Prevention of Cruelty to Animals**
Causeway
Horsham
West Sussex RH12 1HG   phone 0403 64181

World Wide Fund for Nature
Panda House
11–13 Ockford Road
Godalming,
Surrey GU7 1QU   phone 0483 426444

WATCH
Royal Society for Nature Conservation
The Green, Widham Park
Lincoln   LN5 7JR   phone 0522 544400

**International Council
for Bird Preservation**
32 Girton Road
Cambridge   CB3 0PJ   phone 0223 277318

The Humane Research Trust
Brook House
29 Bramhall Lane South
Cheshire   SK7 2DN

**The Jersey Wildlife
Preservation Trust**
Les Augres Manor
Trinity
Jersey
Channel Islands   JE2 6SP   phone 0534 61949

Nature Conservancy Council
Northminster House
Peterborough   PE1 1UA   phone 0733 40345

Greendays notes